PIANO CHORD SONGBOOK

Gospel Hymns

T0081657

ISBN 978-1-4950-3582-1

HAL•LEONARD®
CORPORATION

7777 W. BLUEMOUND RD. P.O. BOX 13819 MILWAUKEE, WI 53213

In Australia Contact:
Hal Leonard Australia Pty. Ltd.
4 Lentara Court
Cheltenham, Victoria, 3192 Australia
Email: ausadmin@halleonard.com.au

Visit Hal Leonard Online at
www.halleonard.com

How to Use This Book

Piano Chord Songbooks include the lyrics and chords for each song. The melody of the first phrase of each song is also shown.

First, play the melody excerpt to get you started in the correct key. Then, sing the song, playing the chords that are shown above the lyrics.

Chords can be voiced in many different ways. For any chords that are unfamiliar, refer to the diagram that is provided for each chord. It shows the notes that you should play with your right hand. With your left hand, simply play the note that matches the name of the chord. For example, to play a C chord, play C-E-G in your right hand, and play a C in your left hand.

You will notice that some chords are *slash chords*; for example, C/G. With your right hand, play the chord that matches the note on the left side of the slash. With your left hand, play the note on the right side of the slash. So, to play a C/G chord, play a C chord (C-E-G) in your right hand, and play a G in your left hand.

Contents

Amazing Grace

Words by John Newton
From *A Collection of Sacred Ballads*
Traditional American Melody
From Carrell and Clayton's *Virginia Harmony*
Arranged by Edwin O. Excell

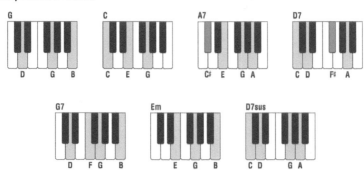

Verse 1

     G   C   G
A - mazing grace, how sweet the sound,

       A7   D7
That saved a wretch like me.

    G G7/B C G
I once was lost but now am found,

     Em D7 G
Was blind but now I see.

Verse 2

     G   C G
'Twas grace that taught my heart to fear,

       A7   D7
And grace my fears re - lieved.

     G G7/B C   G
How precious did that grace ap - pear

    Em D7 G
The hour I first be - lieved.

Verse 3

G   C   G
The Lord has prom - ised good to me,

          A7   D7sus
His word my hope se - cures.

D7 G   G7/B   C   G
He will my shield and portion be

   Em   G D7 G
As long as life en - dures.

Verse 4

           G   C   G
Through many dangers, toils and snares,

        A7   D7
I have al - ready come.

 G   G7/B   C   G
'Tis grace hath brought me safe thus far,

 Em   D7   G
And grace will lead me home.

Verse 5

           G   C   G
When we've been there ten thou - sand years,

        A7   D7
Bright shining as the sun,

   G   G7/B C   G
We've no less days to sing God's praise

   Em   D7 G
Than when we'd first be - gun.

Are You Washed in the Blood?

Words and Music by
Elisha A. Hoffman

Melody:

Have you been to Je-sus for the cleans-ing power?

Verse 1

	G		C/G G
Have you been to Jesus for the cleans - ing   power?

       G   **A7**   **D**
Are you washed in the blood of the lamb?

       G   **C**
Are you fully trusting in His grace this hour?

       G   **D7** **G**
Are you washed in the blood of the Lamb?

Chorus 1

       G   **C**
Are you washed in the blood,

    G   **D G**   **D**
In the soul cleans - ing blood of the Lamb?

  D7 **G**
Are your garments spotless?

      C
Are they white as snow?

      G   **D7** **G**
Are you washed in the blood of the Lamb?

Verse 2	G C/G G

Verse 2

     G   C/G G
Are you walking daily by the Sav - ior's side?

     G   A7   D
Are you washed in the blood of the Lamb?

     G   C
Do you rest each moment in the crucified?

     G   D7   G
Are you washed in the blood of the Lamb?

Chorus 2   *Repeat Chorus 1*

Verse 3

      G   C/G G
When the Bridegroom cometh will your robes be   white?

     G   A7   D
Are you washed in the blood of the Lamb?

      G   C
Will your soul be ready for the mansions bright,

     G   D7   G
And be washed in the blood of the Lamb?

Chorus 3   *Repeat Chorus 1*

Verse 4

     G   C/G G
Lay a - side the garments that are stained with sin,

      G   A7   D
And be washed in the blood of the Lamb.

      G   C
There's a fountain flowing for the soul unclean,

     G   D7   G
O be washed in the blood of the lamb.

Chorus 4   *Repeat Chorus 1*

At Calvary

Words by William R. Newell
Music by Daniel B. Towner

Melody:

Years I spent in van - i - ty and pride,

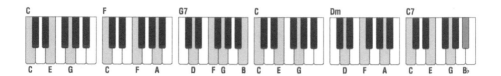

C	F	G7	C	Dm	C7
C E G	C F A	D F G B	C E G	D F A	C E G B♭

Verse 1

   C   F/C C
Years I spent in vanity and pride,

G7   C   F/C C
Caring not my Lord was cru - ci - fied,

                          F/C C C/E Dm/F G7 C
Knowing not it was for me He   died on   Cal - va - ry.

Chorus 1

F   C
Mercy there was great and grace was free,

G7   C   C7/E
Pardon there was multi - plied to me.

F   C C/E Dm/F G7 C
There my burdened soul found lib - erty, at   Cal - va - ry.

Verse 2	C F/C C

Verse 2

C   F/C C
By God's Word at last my sin I learned,

G7   C F/C C
Then I trembled at the law I'd spurned,

       F/C C C/E Dm/F G7 C
Till my guilty soul implor‑ing turned to Cal ‑ va‑ry.

Chorus 2   *Repeat Chorus 1*

Verse 3

C   F/C C
Now I've giv'n to Jesus ev‑'ry‑thing.

G7   C F/C C
Now I gladly own Him as my King.

       F/C C C/E Dm/F G7 C
Now my raptured soul can on‑ly sing of Cal ‑ va‑ry.

Chorus 3   *Repeat Chorus 1*

Verse 4

C   F/C C
O the love that true salva‑tion's plan!

G7   C F/C C
O the grace that brought it down to man.

       F/C C C/E Dm/F G7 C
O the mighty gulf that God did span at Cal ‑ va‑ry.

Chorus 4   *Repeat Chorus 1*

At the Cross

Words by Isaac Watts and Ralph E. Hudson
Music by Ralph E. Hudson

Melody:

A - las! and did my Sav - ior bleed?

D   D   F#   A

G   D   G   B

A7   C# E   G A

A   C# E   A

G6   D E   G   B

Verse 1

        D
A - las! and did my Savior bleed?

D/F# G D/F# A7/E D   A
And   did my   Sov - 'reign die?

D   **G/D D**
Would He devote that sa - cred head

     G6   **D**   **A7 D**
For sinners such as   I?

Chorus 1

             D   **G/D   D**   **A**
At the cross, at the cross where I first ___ saw the light,

      A7   **D**
And the burden of my heart rolled a - way.

      G   **D**
It was there by faith I re - ceived my sight,

      G6   **A7**   **D**
And now I am happy all the day!

Verse 2

       D
Was it for crimes that I have done

D/F♯ G   **D/F♯ A7/E D A**
He   groaned up - on   the tree?

D   **G/D D**
Amazing pity, grace un - known!

    G6   **D**   **A7 D**
And love be - yond de - gree.

Chorus 2   *Repeat Chorus 1*

Verse 3

       D
Well might the sun in darkness hide

D/F♯ G D/F♯ A7/E D A
And   shut His   glo - ries in,

D   **G/D D**
When Christ, the mighty Mak - er,   died

    G6   **D**   **A7** **D**
For man, the crea - ture's sin.

Chorus 3   *Repeat Chorus 1*

Verse 4

       D
But drops of grief can ne'er repay

D/F♯ G D/F♯ A7/E D A
The   debt of   love I owe.

D   **G/D D**
Here, Lord, I give myself a - way,

    G6   **D A7 D**
'Tis all that I   can do!

Chorus 4   *Repeat Chorus 1*

Blessed Assurance

Lyrics by Fanny J. Crosby
Music by Phoebe Palmer Knapp

Bless-ed as - sur-ance, Je-sus is mine! Oh, what a...

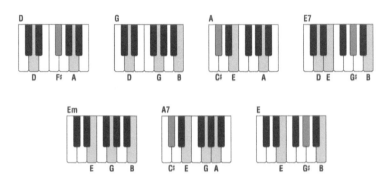

Verse 1

        D   **G**   **D**
Blessed as - surance, Jesus is mine!

       A   **E7**   **A**
Oh, what a fore - taste of glory di - vine!

D   **G**   **D**
Heir of salvation, purchase of God,

     G **Em/G** **D**   **A7**   **D**
Born of His Spir - it,   washed in His blood.

Chorus 1

D   **G**   **D**
This is my story, this is my song,

    G **D/F♯** **A**   **E**   **A**
Praising my Sav - ior   all the day long.

A7   **D**   **G**   **D**
This is my story, this is my song,

    G **Em/G** **D** **A7**   **D**
Praising my Sav - ior   all the day long.

PIANO CHORD SONGBOOK

Verse 2	D G D

Verse 2

      D   G   D
Perfect sub - mission, perfect de - light!

              A   E7   A
Visions of rap - ture now burst on my sight.

D   G   D
Angels descending bring from a - bove

          G   Em/G D   A7   D
Echoes of mer - cy,   whis - pers of love.

Chorus 2   *Repeat Chorus 1*

Verse 3

      D   G   D
Perfect sub - mission, all is at rest,

           A   E7   A
I in my Sav - ior am happy and blessed.

D   G   D
Watching and waiting, looking a - bove,

          G   Em/G D A7   D
Filled with His good - ness,   lost in His love.

Chorus 3   *Repeat Chorus 1*

Blessed Be the Name

Words by Charles Wesley
and Ralph E. Hudson
Traditional
Arranged by Ralph E. Hudson
and William J. Kirkpatrick

Verse 1

    A♭   D♭   A♭
O for a thousand tongues to sing,

              E♭
Blessed by the name of the Lord!

    A♭   D♭   A♭
The glories of my God and King,

          E♭7 A♭
Blessed be the name of the Lord!

Chorus 1

    A♭   D♭   A♭
Blessed be the name! Blessed be the name!

            E♭
Blessed be the name of the Lord!

    A♭   D♭   A♭
Blessed be the name! Blessed be the name!

        E♭   E♭7 A♭
Blessed be the name of the Lord!

PIANO CHORD SONGBOOK

Verse 2

Ab   Db   Ab
Je - sus, the name that charms our fears,

                  Eb
Blessed be the name of the Lord!

Ab   Db   Ab
'Tis music in the sinner's ears,

                Eb7 Ab
Blessed be the name of the Lord!

Chorus 2   *Repeat Chorus 1*

Verse 3

Ab   Db   Ab
He breaks the power of canceled sin,

                  Eb
Blessed be the name of the Lord!

Ab   Db   Ab
His blood can make the foulest clean,

                Eb7 Ab
Blessed be the name of the Lord!

Chorus 3   *Repeat Chorus 1*

Brighten the Corner Where You Are

Words by Ina Duley Ogdon
Music by Charles H. Gabriel

Do not wait un - til some deed of great-ness you may do,

Verse 1

       D   **D/F♯** **Fdim7** **A7/E**
Do not wait until some deed of greatness you   may   do,

       A7   **D**
Do not wait to shed your light a - far.

A7   **D**   **G**
To the many duties ever near you now be true.

D   **A7 D**
Brighten the corner where you are.

Chorus 1

                 A7
Brighten the corner where you are.

                D
Brighten the corner where you are.

                        G
Someone far from harbor you may guide across the bar.

D   **A7 D**
Brighten the corner where you are.

Verse 2

D   D/F♯ Fdim7 A7/E
Just a - bove are clouded skies that you may help   to   clear.

A7   D
Let not narrow self your way de - bar,

A7   D   G
Though in - to one heart alone may fall your song of cheer.

D   A7 D
Brighten the corner where you are.

Chorus 2   *Repeat Chorus 1*

Verse 3

D   D/F♯ Fdim7 A7/E
Here for all your talent you may surely find   a   need.

A7   D
Here re - flect the Bright and Morning Star.

A7 D   G
Even from your humble hand the bread of life may feed.

D   A7 D
Brighten the corner where you are.

Chorus 3   *Repeat Chorus 1*

Church in the Wildwood

Words and Music by
Dr. William S. Pitts

There's a church in the val - ley by the wild - wood,

Verse 1

     B♭ E♭ B♭   F7
There's a church in the valley by the wild - wood,

        B♭
No lovelier spot in the dale.

B♭/D E♭   B♭
No place is so dear to my childhood

    F7   B♭
As the little brown church in the vale.

Chorus 1

    B♭
Oh, come, come, come, come.

    E♭ B♭   F7
Come to the church in the wild - wood,

        B♭
Oh, come to the church in the vale.

B♭/D E♭   B♭
No spot is so dear to my childhood

    F7   B♭
As the little brown church in the vale.

Verse 2

        B♭   **E♭ B♭**   **F7**
Oh, come to the church in the wild - wood,

                   B♭
To the trees where the wild flowers bloom,

B♭/D   **E♭**   **B♭**
Where the parting hymn will be chanted,

    F7   **B♭**
We will weep by the side of the tomb.

Chorus 2   *Repeat Chorus 1*

Verse 3

       B♭   **E♭ B♭**   **F7**
From the church in the valley by the wild - wood,

            B♭
When day fades away into night,

B♭/D **E♭**   **B♭**
I would fain from this spot of my childhood

    F7   **B♭**
Wing my way to the mansions of light.

Chorus 3   *Repeat Chorus 1*

Count Your Blessings

Words by Johnson Oatman, Jr.
Music by Edwin O. Excell

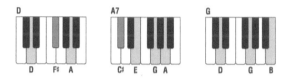

Verse 1

  D   A7
When upon life's billows you are tempest tossed,

                          D
When you are discouraged, thinking all is lost,

                          A7
Count your many blessings, name them one by one,

                D A7 D
And it will surprise you what the Lord hath done.

Chorus 1

D   A7
Count your blessings, name them one by one.

                D
Count your blessings, see what God hath done.

      G   A7   G/A A7
Count your blessings, name them one by one.

D   G   D A7 D
Count your many blessings, see what God hath done.

Verse 2

D   A7
Are you ever burdened with a load of care?

                                    D
Does the cross seem heavy you are called to bear?

                             A7
Count your many blessings, ev'ry doubt will fly,

                           D A7 D
And you will be singing as the days go by.

Chorus 2   *Repeat Chorus 1*

Verse 3

D   A7
When you look at others with their lands and gold,

                                    D
Think that Christ has promised you His wealth untold.

                            A7
Count your many blessings, money cannot buy

                           D   A7 D
Your reward in heaven nor your home on high.

Chorus 3   *Repeat Chorus 1*

Verse 4

D   A7
So amid the conflict, whether great or small,

                                 D
Do not be discouraged, God is over all.

                             A7
Count your many blessings, angels will attend,

                           D   A7 D
Help and comfort give you to your jour - ney's end.

Chorus 4   *Repeat Chorus 1*

Does Jesus Care?

Words by Frank E. Graeff
Music by J. Lincoln Hall

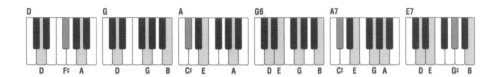

Verse 1

      D   **G/D**   **D**   **G/D D**
Does Jesus care when my heart is   pained

   A   **D**
Too deeply for mirth and song;

                     G6
As the burdens press, and the cares distress,

     D   **A7**   **D**
And the way grows weary and long?

Chorus 1

   A7   **D**
O yes, He cares, I know He cares.

   A   **E7**   **A D A7**
His heart is touched with my grief.

     D   **G6**
When the days are weary, the long nights dreary,

   D   **A7**   **D G/D D**
I know my Savior cares.

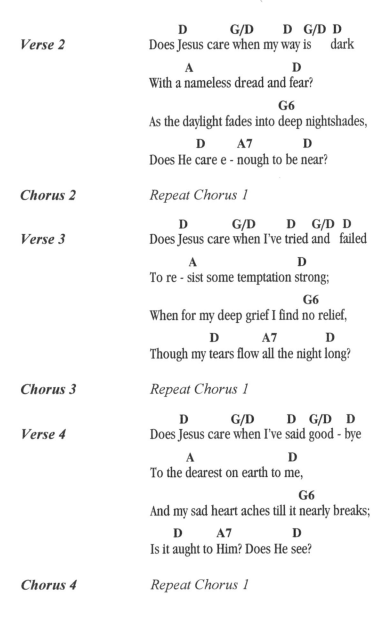

Verse 2

   D **G/D** **D** **G/D** **D**
Does Jesus care when my way is dark

   A   **D**
With a nameless dread and fear?

        G6
As the daylight fades into deep nightshades,

   D **A7**   **D**
Does He care e - nough to be near?

Chorus 2   *Repeat Chorus 1*

Verse 3

   D **G/D** **D** **G/D** **D**
Does Jesus care when I've tried and failed

   A   **D**
To re - sist some temptation strong;

        G6
When for my deep grief I find no relief,

    D **A7**   **D**
Though my tears flow all the night long?

Chorus 3   *Repeat Chorus 1*

Verse 4

   D **G/D** **D** **G/D** **D**
Does Jesus care when I've said good - bye

   A   **D**
To the dearest on earth to me,

        G6
And my sad heart aches till it nearly breaks;

   D **A7**   **D**
Is it aught to Him? Does He see?

Chorus 4   *Repeat Chorus 1*

Down At the Cross
(Glory to His Name)

Words by Elisha A. Hoffman
Music by John H. Stockton

Verse 1

G   G/B   C   G
Down at the cross where my Sav - ior died,

                                D
Down where for cleansing from sin I cried,

G   G/B   C   G
There to my heart was the blood ap - plied;

G/D   D7 G
Glory to His name!

Chorus 1

C   G
Glory to His name!

         D
Glory to His name!

G   G/B   C   G
There to my heart was the blood ap - plied.

      D7 G
Glory to His name.

PIANO CHORD SONGBOOK

Verse 2

```
G            G/B   C      G
I am so won - drously saved from sin,

                           D
Jesus so sweetly abides with - in;

G                G/B   C      G
There at the cross where He took me in;

G/D     D7 G
Glory to His name!
```

Chorus 2   *Repeat Chorus 1*

Verse 3

```
G                G/B   C       G
O precious foun - tain that saves from sin,

                           D
I am so glad that I entered in;

G                G/B   C      G
There Jesus saves me and keeps me clean;

G/D     D7 G
Glory to His name!
```

Chorus 3   *Repeat Chorus 1*

Verse 4

```
G                G/B   C      G
Come to this foun - tain so rich and sweet;

                           D
Cast thy poor soul at the Savior's feet;

G            G/B   C          G
Plunge in today and be made com - plete;

G/D     D7 G
Glory to His name!
```

Chorus 4   *Repeat Chorus 1*

Down by the Riverside

African-American Spiritual

Gon -na lay down my bur - den... _

Verse 1

        G
Gonna lay down my burden

               D7
Down by the riverside,

              G
Down by the riverside,

Down by the riverside.

Gonna lay down my burden

Down by the riverside

D7   **G**
And study war no more.

Chorus 1

             C
I ain't gonna study war no more,

             G
I ain't gonna study war no more,

             D7   **G**
I ain't gonna study war no more.

             C
I ain't gonna study war no more,

             G
I ain't gonna study war no more,

             D7   **G**
I ain't gonna study war no more.

Verse 2

       G
Gonna lay down my sword and shield

      D7
Down by the riverside,

      G
Down by the riverside,

Down by the riverside.

Gonna lay down my sword and shield

Down by the riverside

 D7   **G**
And study war no more.

Chorus 2   *Repeat Chorus 1*

Verse 3

     G
Gonna try on my long white robe

      D7
Down by the riverside,

      G
Down by the riverside,

Down by the riverside.

Gonna try on my long white robe

Down by the riverside

 D7   **G**
And study war no more.

Chorus 3   *Repeat Chorus 1*

Dwelling in Beulah Land

Words and Music by
C. Austin Miles

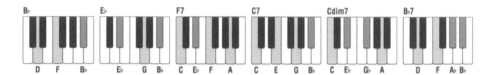

Verse 1

Bb   Eb Bb Eb Bb
Far away the noise of strife

      F7   Bb
Upon my ear is falling.

Eb   Bb   C7   F7
Then I know the sins of earth be - set on ev'ry hand.

Bb   Eb Bb   Eb Bb
Doubt and fear and things of earth

      F7   Bb
In vain to me are calling.

Eb   Bb/D   Eb Bb F7 Bb
None of these shall move me from Beu - lah Land.

Chorus 1

Bb Eb Bb   C°7   F7/C
I'm living on the mountain, underneath a cloudless sky.

  F7   Bb   C7   F7
I'm drinking at the fountain that never shall run dry.

      Bb   Bb7 Eb   Bb
O yes, I'm feasting on the manna from a bountiful sup - ply,

      Eb Bb F7 Bb
For I am dwelling in Beu - lah Land.

PIANO CHORD SONGBOOK

Verse 2

Bb   Eb Bb   Eb Bb
Far below the storm of doubt

          F7   Bb
Upon the world is beating.

Eb   Bb   C7   F7
Sons of men in battle long the enemy with - stand.

Bb   Eb   Bb Eb Bb
Safe am I with - in the castle

          F7   Bb
Of God's Word re - treating,

Eb   Bb/D   Eb Bb   F7 Bb
Nothing then can reach me; 'tis Beu - lah Land.

Chorus 2

Repeat Chorus 1

Verse 3

Bb   Eb Bb   Eb Bb
Let the storm - y breez - es blow,

          F7   Bb
Their cry can - not a - larm me.

Eb   Bb   C7   F7
I am safely sheltered here, pro - tected by God's hand.

Bb   Eb Bb Eb Bb
Here the sun is al - ways shining,

          F7   Bb
Here there's naught can harm me.

Eb   Bb/D Eb Bb   F7 Bb
I am safe for - ever in Beu - lah Land.

Chorus 3   *Repeat Chorus 1*

Verse 4

        B♭   **E♭ B♭**   **E♭ B♭**
Viewing here the works of God,

             F7   **B♭**
I sink in contem - plation.

        E♭   **B♭**   **C7**   **F7**
Hearing now His blessed voice, I see the way He planned.

        B♭   **E♭ B♭**   **E♭**
Dwelling in the Spir - it,

        B♭   **F7**   **B♭**
Here I learn of full sal - vation,

        E♭   **B♭/D E♭ B♭**   **F7 B♭**
Gladly will I tarry in Beu - lah Land.

Chorus 4   *Repeat Chorus 1*

Give Me That Old Time Religion

Traditional

Verse 1

               B♭
Give me that old time religion,

           F7   **B♭**
Give me that old time re - ligion,

          B♭7   **E♭**
Give me that old time re - ligion,

     B♭   **F7**   **B♭**
It's good e - nough for me.

Verse 2

               B♭
It was good for our fathers,

           F7   **B♭**
It was good for our fathers,

         B♭7   **E♭**
It was good for our fathers,

      B♭   **F7**   **B♭**
And it's good e - nough for me.

Verse 3

               B♭
It was good for our mothers,

           F7   **B♭**
It was good for our mothers,

         B♭7   **E♭**
It was good for our mothers,

      B♭   **F7**   **B♭**
And it's good e - nough for me.

Verse 4   *Repeat Verse 1*

The Eastern Gate

Words and Music by
Isaiah G. Martin

Melody:

I will meet you in the morn - ing,

G   C   D7   D

Verse 1

         G   C   G
I will meet you in the morning, just inside the Eastern Gate;

                         C   D7   G
Then be ready, faithful pilgrim, lest with you it be too late.

Chorus 1

                  G
I will meet you in the morning, I will meet you in the morning,

                                D
Just inside the Eastern Gate over there.

                  G
I will meet you in the morning, I will meet you in the morning,

                         D7   G
I will meet you in the morning over there.

	G	C	G
Verse 2	If you hasten off to glory, linger near the Eastern Gate;		

	C	D7	G
	For I'm coming in the morning, so you'll not have long to wait.		

Chorus 2   *Repeat Chorus 1*

	G
Verse 3	Keep your lamps all trimmed and burning,

	C	G
	For the Bridegroom watch and wait.	

	C	D7	G
	He'll be with us at the meeting, just inside the Eastern Gate!		

Chorus 3   *Repeat Chorus 1*

	G	C	G
Verse 4	O the joy of that glad meeting with the saints who for us wait!		

	C	D7	G
	What a blessed happy meeting, just inside the Eastern Gate!		

Chorus 4   *Repeat Chorus 1*

Footsteps of Jesus

Words by Mary B.C. Slade
Music by Asa B. Everett

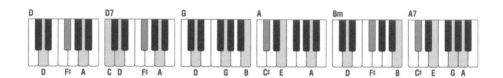

Verse 1

   D   D7   G   D
Sweetly, Lord, have we heard Thee call - ing,

               A
"Come, follow Me!"

   D   D7   G   D
And we see where Thy footprints fall - ing

Bm D A7 D
Lead us to Thee.

Chorus 1

   G   D   G/D D   A
Footprints of Je - sus, that make the pathway glow.

   D   D7   G   D
We will fol - low the steps of Je - sus

Bm   D   A7   D
Wher - e'er they go.

Verse 2

```
D              D7      G            D
Though the lead o'er the cold, dark moun - tains,

            A
Seeking His sheep,

D      D7    G          D
Or along by Si - loam's foun - tains,

Bm    D  A7  D
Help - ing the  weak.
```

Chorus 2   *Repeat Chorus 1*

Verse 3

```
D           D7         G          D
If they lead through the temple ho - ly,

            A
Preaching the Word,

D        D7   G           D
Or in homes of the poor and low - ly,

Bm    D  A7  D
Serv - ing the  Lord.
```

Chorus 3   *Repeat Chorus 1*

Verse 4

```
D           D7         G          D
Then at last, when on high He sees us,

            A
Our journey done,

D           D7      G           D
We will rest where the steps of Je - sus

Bm  D A7  D
End  at  His  throne.
```

Chorus 4   *Repeat Chorus 1*

God Will Take Care of You

Words by Civilla D. Martin
Music by W. Stillman Martin

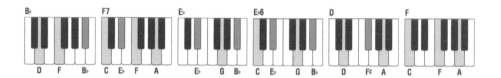

Verse 1

Bb   F7 Bb
Be not dismayed whate'er be - tide,

F7   Bb
God will take care of you.

          F7 Bb
Beneath His wings of love a - bide,

F7   Bb
God will take care of you.

Chorus 1

Eb   Bb
God will take care of you,

F7   Bb
Through ev'ry day, o'er all the way.

  Bb/D Eb6 D
He will take care of you,

Eb   Bb F Bb
God will take care of you.

Verse 2	**Bb** **F7** **Bb** Through days of toil when heart doth fail,

Verse 2

Bb   **F7** **Bb**
Through days of toil when heart doth fail,

F7   **Bb**
God will take care of you.

                                F7 **Bb**
When dangers fierce your path as - sail,

F7   **Bb**
God will take care of you.

Chorus 2   *Repeat Chorus 1*

Verse 3

Bb   **F7** **Bb**
All you may need He will pro - vide,

F7   **Bb**
God will take care of you.

                              F7 **Bb**
Nothing you ask will be de - nied,

F7   **Bb**
God will take care of you.

Chorus 3   *Repeat Chorus 1*

Verse 4

Bb   **F7** **Bb**
No matter what may be the test,

F7   **Bb**
God will take care of you.

                              F7 **Bb**
Lean, weary one, upon His breast,

F7   **Bb**
God will take care of you.

Chorus 4   *Repeat Chorus 1*

Hallelujah, We Shall Rise

By J.E. Thomas

Verse 1

      A
In the resurrection morning, when the trump of God shall sound,
     F#m7 B9   E7   A
(We shall rise.) Halle - lujah! We shall rise.

Then the saints will come rejoicing and no tears will e'er be found.

Chorus 1

     A F#m7 B9   E7   A
We shall rise, halle - lujah! In the morning, we shall rise.

(We shall rise.) Hallelujah! (We shall rise.) Amen.

                D   **A**
(We shall rise.) Hallelujah! In the resurrection morn - ing

When death's prison bars are broken,
     F#m7 B9   E7   A
We shall rise, halle - lujah! We shall rise.

PIANO CHORD SONGBOOK

Verse 2

A

In the resurrection morning, what a meeting it will be.

F#m7 B9   E7   A

(We shall rise.) Halle - lujah! We shall rise!

When our fathers and our mothers and our loved ones we shall see.

Chorus 2   *Repeat Chorus 1*

Verse 3

A

In the resurrection morning, blessed thought it is to me.

F#m7 B9   E7   A

(We shall rise.) Halle - lujah! We shall rise.

I shall see my blessed Savior, who so freely died for me.

Chorus 3   *Repeat Chorus 1*

Verse 4

A

In the resurrection morning, we shall meet Him in the air.

F#m7 B9   E7   A

(We shall rise.) Halle - lujah! We shall rise.

And be carried up to glory, to our home so bright and fair.

Chorus 4   *Repeat Chorus 1*

He Hideth My Soul

Words by Fanny J. Crosby
Music by William J. Kirkpatrick

A won-der-ful Sav-ior is Je-sus, my Lord,

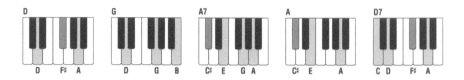

Verse 1

    D   G   D
A wonderful Savior is Jesus, my Lord,

             A7 D A
A wonderful Sav - ior to me.

A7 D   G
He   hideth my soul in the cleft of the rock,

       D   A   A7 D
Where rivers of pleasure I   see.

Chorus 1

    A7   D   G/D D
He hideth my soul in the cleft of the   rock

    A7   A/C♯ D
That shadows a dry, thirst - y   land.

          D7 G
He hideth my life in the depths of His love

    D   A   D A7 D A7 D
And covers me there with His hand,

G D   A7   D
And covers me there with His hand.

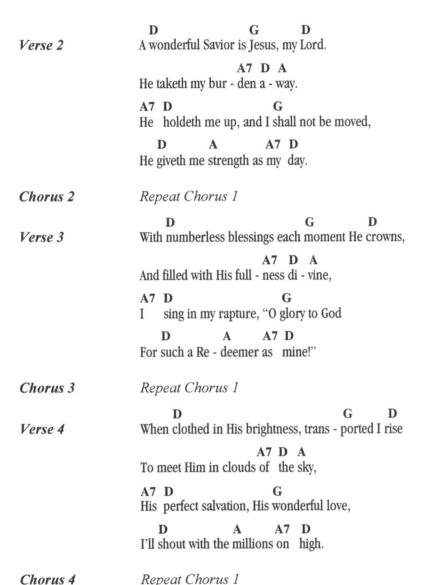

Verse 2

```
       D            G      D
A wonderful Savior is Jesus, my Lord.

              A7  D  A
He taketh my bur - den a - way.

A7  D              G
He   holdeth me up, and I shall not be moved,

      D        A      A7  D
He giveth me strength as my  day.
```

Chorus 2   *Repeat Chorus 1*

Verse 3

```
        D                    G      D
With numberless blessings each moment He crowns,

              A7   D  A
And filled with His full - ness di - vine,

A7  D                 G
I     sing in my rapture, "O glory to God

      D        A      A7  D
For such a Re - deemer as   mine!"
```

Chorus 3   *Repeat Chorus 1*

Verse 4

```
        D                    G     D
When clothed in His brightness, trans - ported I rise

              A7  D  A
To meet Him in clouds of   the sky,

A7  D                 G
His  perfect salvation, His wonderful love,

      D          A      A7  D
I'll shout with the millions on   high.
```

Chorus 4   *Repeat Chorus 1*

He Keeps Me Singing

Words and Music by
Luther B. Bridgers

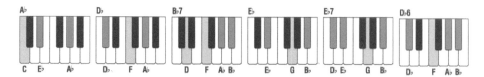

Verse 1

Aᵇ   Dᵇ Aᵇ Bᵇ7
There's within my heart a melody,

Eᵇ   Aᵇ Eᵇ7
Jesus whispers sweet and low:

Aᵇ   Dᵇ Aᵇ Bᵇ7
"Fear not, I am with thee, peace, be still,"

Eᵇ   Aᵇ Eᵇ7 Aᵇ
In all of life's ebb and flow.

Chorus 1

Aᵇ   Aᵇ/C Eᵇ7/Bᵇ Eᵇ
Jesus, Je - sus, Je - sus,

            Aᵇ
Sweetest name I know.

       Aᵇ/C Dᵇ6 Dᵇ
Fills my ev - 'ry   long - ing,

Eᵇ   Aᵇ Eᵇ7 Aᵇ
Keeps me singing as I go.

Verse 2

Aᵇ   Dᵇ   Aᵇ Bᵇ7
All my life was wrecked by sin and strife,

Eᵇ   Aᵇ Eᵇ7
Discord filled my heart with pain.

Aᵇ   Dᵇ Aᵇ Bᵇ7
Jesus swept a - cross the broken strings,

Eᵇ   Aᵇ Eᵇ7 Aᵇ
Stirred the slumb'ring chords a - gain.

Chorus 2

Repeat Chorus 1

Verse 3

$A\flat$ $D\flat$ $A\flat$ $B\flat7$
Feasting on the rich - es of His grace,

$E\flat$ $A\flat$ $E\flat7$
Resting 'neath His shelt'ring wing,

$A\flat$ $D\flat$ $A\flat$ $B\flat7$
Always looking on His smiling face,

$E\flat$ $A\flat$ $E\flat7$ $A\flat$
That is why I shout and sing.

Chorus 3   *Repeat Chorus 1*

Verse 4

$A\flat$ $D\flat$ $A\flat$ $B\flat7$
Though sometimes He leads through waters deep,

$E\flat$ $A\flat$ $E\flat7$
Trials fall across the way,

$A\flat$ $D\flat$ $A\flat$ $B\flat7$
Though sometimes the path seems rough and steep,

$E\flat$ $A\flat$ $E\flat7$ $A\flat$
See His footprints all the way.

Chorus 4   *Repeat Chorus 1*

Verse 5

$A\flat$ $D\flat$ $A\flat$ $B\flat7$
Soon He's coming back to welcome me

$E\flat$ $A\flat$ $E\flat7$
Far beyond the starry sky.

$A\flat$ $D\flat$ $A\flat$ $B\flat7$
I shall wing my flight to worlds unknown,

$E\flat$ $A\flat$ $E\flat7$ $A\flat$
I shall reign with Him on high.

Chorus 5   *Repeat Chorus 1*

He's Got the Whole World in His Hands

Traditional Spiritual

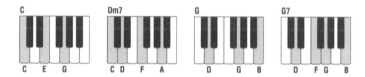

                C
Chorus 1   He's got the whole world in His hands,

                Dm7   **G**   **Dm7**   **G7**
               He's got the whole wide world in His hands,

                C
               He's got the whole world in His hands,

                G7   **C**
               He's got the whole world in His hands.

                C
Verse 1   He's got the little tiny baby in His hands,

                Dm7   **G7** **Dm7**   **G7**
               He's got the little tiny baby in His hands,

                C
               He's got the little tiny baby in His hands,

                G7   **C**
               He's got the whole world in His hands.

Chorus 2   *Repeat Chorus 1*

Verse 2
```
                 C
He's got you and me, brother, in His hands,
        Dm7        G7   Dm7      G7
He's got you and me, sister, in His hands,
                 C
He's got you and me, brother, in His hands,
        G7               C
He's got the whole world in His hands.
```

Chorus 3   *Repeat Chorus 1*

Verse 3
```
                 C
He's got ev'rybody here in His hands,
        Dm7    G7  Dm7       G7
He's got ev'rybody here in His hands,
                 C
He's got ev'rybody here in His hands,
        G7               C
He's got the whole world in His hands.
```

Chorus 4   *Repeat Chorus 1*

Heavenly Sunlight

Words by Henry J. Zelley
Music by George Harrison Cook

Melody:

Walk-ing in sun - light all of my jour - ney,

G
D
G
B
C
E
G
A7
C♯
E
G
A
D7
C
D
F♯
A
D
D
F♯
A

Verse 1

       G   D
Walking in sunlight all of my journey,

G C/G G   A7   D
O - ver the mountains, through the deep vale;

        G   D
Jesus has said, "I'll never for - sake thee,"

G   C/G G   D7 G/D D7 G
Prom - ise divine that nev - er   can fail.

Chorus 1

          C   C/E G/D C G
Heavenly sunlight, heav - en - ly sunlight,

                  A7   D
Flooding my soul with glory di - vine.

       G   D
Halle - lujah! I am re - joicing,

G   C/G G   D7 G/D D7 G
Sing - ing His praises, Je - sus is mine.

PIANO CHORD SONGBOOK

Verse 2

           G   **D**
Shadows a - round me, shadows a - bove me,

G **C/G** **G**   **A7**   **D**
Nev - er   conceal my Savior and Guide.

           G   **D**
He is the light, in Him is no darkness.

G **C/G** **G**   **D7** **G/D** **D7** **G**
Ev - er   I'm walking close to   His side.

Chorus 2   *Repeat Chorus 1*

Verse 3

           G   **D**
In the bright sunlight, ever re - joicing,

G **C/G** **G**   **A7**   **D**
Press - ing my way to mansions a - bove.

           G   **D**
Singing His praises, gladly I'm walking,

G **C/G** **G**   **D7** **G/D** **D7** **G**
Walk - ing in sunlight, sun - light of love.

Chorus 3   *Repeat Chorus 1*

Higher Ground

Words by Johnson Oatman, Jr.
Music by Charles H. Gabriel

I'm press-ing   on   the   up-ward   way,

Verse 1

     G   C
I'm pressing on the upward way,

       G   D
New heights I'm gaining ev'ry day.

    G   C
Still praying as I'm onward bound,

       G   D7 G
"Lord, plant my feet on high - er   ground."

Chorus 1

       G   D7
Lord, lift me up and let me stand,

          G
By faith, on heaven's table - land,

        D/A G/B   C
A higher plane than I   have found.

      G   D7 G
Lord, plant my feet on high - er   ground.

Verse 2

                G   C
My heart has no desire to stay

                     G   D
Where doubts a - rise and fears dis - may.

            G   C
Though some may dwell where these a - bound,

                G   D7 G
My prayer, my aim, is high - er   ground.

Chorus 2   *Repeat Chorus 1*

Verse 3

                G   C
I want to live above the world,

                     G   D
Though Satan's darts at me are hurled.

            G   C
For faith has caught the joyful sound,

                G   D7 G
The song of saints on high - er ground.

Chorus 3   *Repeat Chorus 1*

Verse 4

                G   C
I want to scale the utmost height,

                     G   D
And catch a gleam of glory bright.

            G   C
But still I'll pray till heav'n I've found,

                G   D7 G
"Lord, lead me on to high - er   ground."

Chorus 4   *Repeat Chorus 1*

His Eye Is on the Sparrow

Words by Civilla D. Martin
Music by Charles H. Gabriel

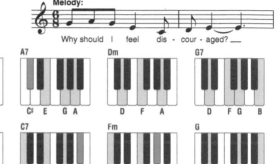

Verse 1

    C
Why should I feel discouraged?

F   **C**
Why should the shadows come?

A7   **Dm**
Why should my heart be lonely

G7   **C**
And long for heav'n and home

When Jesus is my portion?
G7 **C**   **F A7**
  My constant Friend is He.

Chorus 1

Dm G7   **C**
  His eye is on the sparrow,

C♯dim7 Dm7   **G7**   **C**
  And I   know He watches me.

G7/D C/E C7   **F**
  His   eye is on the sparrow,

Fm   **C**   **G7**   **C**
  And I know He watches me.

 G   **C**
I sing because I'm happy,

 G   **C**
I sing because I'm free.

             C7/E **F**
For His eye is on the sparrow,

Fm   **C**   **G7 C**
  And I know He watch - es me.

Verse 2

C
"Let not your heart be troubled,"

F   C
His tender words I hear,

A7   Dm
And, resting on His goodness,

G7   C
I lose my doubt and fear.

Though by the path He leadeth

G7   C   F A7
But one step I may see.

Chorus 2   *Repeat Chorus 1*

Verse 3

C
Whenever I am tempted,

F   C
Whenever clouds a - rise,

A7   Dm
When songs give place to sighing,

G7   C
When hope within me dies,

I draw the closer to Him,

G7   C   F A7
From care He sets me free.

Chorus 3   *Repeat Chorus 1*

I Feel Like Traveling On

Words by William Hunter
Traditional Melody
Music Arranged by James D. Vaughan

My — heav-en - ly home — is — bright and fair,

D G B   C D F♯ A

Verse 1

    G   D7
My heavenly home is bright and fair, I feel like traveling on.
    G   D7   G
No pain or death can enter there, I feel like traveling on.

Chorus 1

          G
Yes, I feel like traveling on,
             D7
I feel like traveling on.
    G
My heavenly home is bright and fair,
      D7   G
I feel like traveling on.

Verse 2

    G   D7
Its glitt'ring towers the sun outshine, I feel like traveling on.
    G   D7   G
That heav'nly mansion shall be mine, I feel like traveling on.

Chorus 2   *Repeat Chorus 1*

Verse 3

    G   D7
Let others seek a home below, I feel like traveling on.
          G   D7   G
Which flames devour or waves o'erflow, I feel like traveling on.

Chorus 3   *Repeat Chorus 1*

Verse 4

    G   D7
The Lord has been so good to me, I feel like traveling on.
    G   D7   G
Un - til that blessed home I see, I feel like traveling on.

Chorus 4   *Repeat Chorus 1*

Life's Railway to Heaven

Words by M.E. Abbey
Music by Charles D. Tillman

Verse 1

     G   D7   G
Life is like a mountain railroad,

      C   G
With an engineer that's brave.

We must make the run successful

    A   D7
From the cradle to the grave.

    G   D7   G
Watch the curves, the fills, the tunnels,

    C   G
Never falter, never quail.

Keep your hand upon the throttle,

    G   D7   G
And your eye up - on the rail.

Chorus 1

      C   G
Blessed Savior, Thou wilt guide us

      A7   D7
Till we reach that blissful shore

    G   C
Where the angels wait to join us

   G   D7   G
In Thy praise for - ever - more.

Verse 2

    G   D7   G
You will roll up grades of trial,

    C   G
You will cross the bridge of strife.

See that Christ is your conductor

    A   D7
On this lightning train of life.

    G   D7   G
Always mindful of ob - struction,

    C   G
Do your duty, never fail.

Keep your hand upon the throttle,

    G   D7   G
And your eye up - on the rail.

Chorus 2   *Repeat Chorus 1*

Verse 3

    G   D7   G
You will often find ob - structions,

    C   G
Look for storms of wind and rain.

On a fill, or curve, or trestle

    A   D7
They will almost ditch your train.

    G   D7   G
Put your trust a - lone in Jesus,

    C   G
Never falter, never fail.

Keep your hand upon the throttle,

    G   D7   G
And your eye up - on the rail.

Chorus 3   *Repeat Chorus 1*

Verse 4

G   D7   G
As you roll a - cross the trestle

     C   G
Spanning Jordan's swelling tide,

You behold the Union Depot

   A   D7
Into which your train will glide.

     G   D7   G
There you'll meet the Sup'rin - tendent,

     C   G
God the Father, God the Son.

With the hearty, joyous plaudit,

    G   D7   G
"Weary pilgrim, welcome home."

Chorus 4   *Repeat Chorus 1*

I Have Decided to Follow Jesus

Folk Melody from India
Arranged by Auila Read

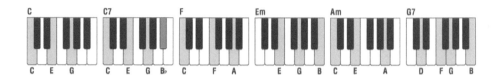

Verse 1

        C
I have de - cided to follow Jesus.

C7   **F**   **C**
I have de - cided to follow Je - sus.

                   Em **Am**
I have decided to follow Je - sus.

           C   **G7**   **C**
No turning back, no turning back.

Verse 2

              C
The world be - hind me, the cross before me.

C7   **F**   **C**
The world be - hind me, the cross before me.

                     Em **Am**
The world behind me, the cross be - fore me.

           C   **G7**   **C**
No turning back, no turning back.

Verse 3

                C
Though none go with me, still I will follow.

   C7   **F**   **C**
Though none go with me, still I will fol - low.

                       Em **Am**
Though none go with me, still I will fol - low.

       C   **G7**   **C**
No turning back, no turning back.

Verse 4

            C
Will you de - cide now to follow Jesus?

   C7   **F**   **C**
Will you de - cide now to follow Je - sus?

                  Em **Am**
Will you decide now to follow Je - sus?

       C   **G7**   **C**
No turning back, no turning back.

I Love to Tell the Story

Words by A. Catherine Hankey
Music by William G. Fischer

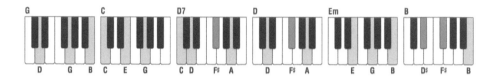

Verse 1

G   G/B C   G
I love to tell the story of   unseen things a - bove,

D7   G   G/B D
Of Jesus and His glo - ry, of Jesus and His love.

D/F# D7   G   Em   B
I love to tell the story be - cause I know 'tis true;

C   G G/B D7   G/D D7   G
It satisfies my long - ings as   noth - ing else can do.

Chorus 1

D7   G
I love to tell the sto - ry.

G/B C   G
'Twill be my theme in glo - ry

G/B   C
To tell the old, old sto - ry

G   D7   G
Of Jesus and His love.

Verse 2

G   G/B C   G
I love to tell the story, more wonderful it seems

        D7   G   G/B D
Than all the golden fan - cies of all our gold - en   dreams.

D/F♯ D7   G   Em   B
I love to tell the story, it did so much for me;

       C   G G/B D7 G/D D7   G
And that is just the rea - son I   tell it   now to thee.

Chorus 2   *Repeat Chorus 1*

Verse 3

G   G/B C   G
I love to tell the story, 'tis   pleasant to re - peat

        D7   G   G/B D
What seems, each time I tell it, more wonderful - ly   sweet.

D/F♯ D7   G   Em   B
I love to tell the story, for some have never heard

       C   G G/B D7   G/D D7 G
The message of salva - tion from God's own holy Word.

Chorus 3   *Repeat Chorus 1*

Verse 4

G   G/B C   G
I love to tell the story, for   those who know it best

        D7   G   G/B D
Seem hungering and thirst - ing to hear it like the   rest.

D/F♯   D7   G   Em   B
And when, in scenes of glory, I sing the new, new song,

       C   G G/B D7 G/D D7   G
'Twill be the old, old sto - ry that I   have loved so long.

Chorus 4   *Repeat Chorus 1*

I Must Tell Jesus

Words and Music by
Elisha A. Hoffman

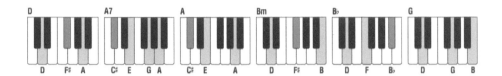

Verse 1

     D   **A7 D**
I must tell Jesus all of my tri - als;

                  A
I cannot bear these burdens a - lone.

D   **A7 Bm**
In my distress He kindly will help me,

B♭   **D**   **A7 D**
He ever loves and cares for His own.

Chorus 1

     D   **D/F♯**   **G**
I must tell Jesus! I must tell Jesus!

      D   **A/C♯** **D A**
I cannot bear my burdens a - lone.

D   **A7 Bm**
I must tell Jesus! I must tell Je - sus!

B♭   **D**   **A7 D**
Jesus can help me, Jesus a - lone.

Verse 2

      D   **A7** **D**
I must tell Jesus all of my trou - bles;

                 A
He is a kind, compassionate Friend.

D   **A7 Bm**
If I but ask Him, He will de - liv - er,

B♭   **D**   **A7** **D**
Make of my troubles quickly an   end.

Chorus 2   *Repeat Chorus 1*

Verse 3

      D   **A7** **D**
O how the world to evil al - lures me!

                 A
O how my heart is tempted to sin!

D   **A7 Bm**
I must tell Jesus, and He will help me

B♭   **D**   **A7 D**
Over the world the vict'ry to   win.

Chorus 3   *Repeat Chorus 1*

I Stand Amazed in the Presence
(My Savior's Love)

Words and Music by
Charles H. Gabriel

Verse 1

    Ab   **Eb**
I stand amazed in the presence of Jesus,

    Ab Eb7 Ab
The Naz - a - rene,

     Db   **Ab Ab/C**
And wonder how He could love me,

Db6 Ab   **Eb7**   **Ab**
A   sinner, con - demned, un - clean.

Chorus 1

Ab
How marvelous! How wonderful!

Eb
And my song shall ever be,

Ab
How marvelous! How wonderful

Db6 Ab   **Eb7 Ab**
Is my Savior's love for me.

Verse 2

    Ab   **Eb**
For me it was in the garden He prayed,

    Ab Eb7 Ab
"Not My will, but Thine."

    Db   **Ab Ab/C**
He had no tears for His own griefs,

Db6 Ab   **Eb7**   **Ab**
But   sweat drops of blood for mine.

Chorus 2   *Repeat Chorus 1*

Verse 3

     A♭
In pity angels beheld Him,

      E♭   A♭ E♭7 A♭
And came from the world of light

      D♭   A♭ A♭/C
To comfort Him in the sor - rows

D♭6 A♭   E♭7   A♭
He   bore for my soul that night.

Chorus 3   *Repeat Chorus 1*

     A♭
Verse 4   He took my sins and my sorrows,

      E♭   A♭ E♭7 A♭
He made them His ver - y   own.

      D♭   A♭ A♭/C
He bore the burden to Cal - v'ry,

D♭6 A♭   E♭7   A♭
And suffered and died a - lone.

Chorus 4   *Repeat Chorus 1*

      A♭
Verse 5   When with the ransomed in glory

      E♭   A♭ E♭7 A♭
His face I at last shall see,

         D♭   A♭ A♭/C
'Twill be my joy through the ag - es

D♭6 A♭   E♭7   A♭
To   sing of His love for me.

Chorus 5   *Repeat Chorus 1*

I've Got Peace Like a River

Traditional

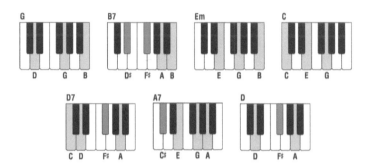

Verse 1

    G
I've got peace like a river,

B7   Em   C   D7
I've got peace like a river,

    G Em A7   D D7
I've got peace like a river in my soul;

    G
I've got peace like a river,

B7   Em   C   .D7
I've got peace like a river,

    G Em A7 D7 G
I've got peace like a river in my soul.

Verse 2

G
I've got love like an ocean,

B7   Em C   D7
I've got love like an ocean,

        G Em A7   D D7
I've got love like an ocean in my soul;

        G
I've got love like an ocean,

B7   Em C   D7
I've got love like an ocean,

        G Em A7 D7 G
I've got love like an ocean in my soul.

Verse 3

        G
I've got joy like a fountain,

B7   Em C   D7
I've got joy like a fountain,

        G Em A7   D D7
I've got joy like a fountain in my soul;

        G
I've got joy like a fountain,

B7   Em C   D7
I've got joy like a fountain,

        G Em A7   D7 G
I've got joy like a fountain in my soul.

In the Garden

Words and Music by
C. Austin Miles

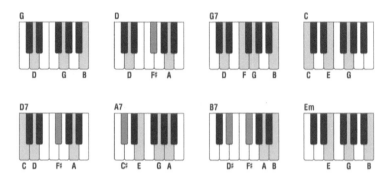

Verse 1

     G   **G/B D G**
I come to the gar - den a - lone,

     G7/B C   **G**
While the   dew is still on the roses.

       D7   **G/B D G**
And the voice I hear, falling on   my ear,

     A7   **D A7 D7**
The Son of God dis - clos - es.

Chorus 1

       G   **D7**
And He walks with me, and He talks with me,

         G
And He tells me I am His own.

       B7   **Em G7/D C**
And the joy we share as we tar - ry   there

     G   **D7 G**
None other has ever known.

Verse 2

G   G/B D G
He speaks, and the sound of His voice

G7/B C   G
Is so sweet the birds hush their singing.

  D7   G/B D G
And the melody that He gave to me

  A7   D A7 D7
With - in my heart is ring - ing.

Chorus 2   *Repeat Chorus 1*

Verse 3

  G   G/B D G
I'd stay in the gar - den with Him

   G7/B C   G
Though the night around me be falling.

  D7   G/B D G
But He bids me go; through the voice of woe,

  A7   D A7 D7
His voice to me is call - ing.

Chorus 3   *Repeat Chorus 1*

Jesus Is the Sweetest Name I Know

Words and Music by
Lela Long

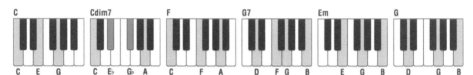

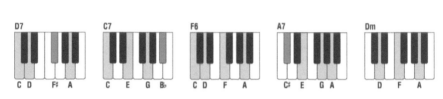

Verse 1

        C   Cdim7 C F   C   G7/F C/E
There have been names   that I have loved to   hear,

C   Cdim7 C   F   G7 C
But never has   there been a name so   dear

G7 Em/G G7   Em/G G7
To this   heart of   mine

C F   C
As the name divine,

     G   D7   G7
The precious, precious name of Je - sus.

Chorus 1

C   Cdim7 C F   C
Jesus is   the sweetest name I know,

         Em/G G7   F   C
And He's just   the same as His love - ly name.

          Cdim7 C F   C
And that's the rea - son why I love Him so,

C7 F6   A7 Dm   G   C
For Jesus is the sweetest name I know.

Verse 2

      C   Cdim7 C F   C   G7/F C/E
There is no name   in earth or heav'n a - bove

C   Cdim7 C F   G7 C
That we should give   such honor and such love

G7 Em/G G7   Em/G G7
As   the   bless - ed   name.

C F   C
Let us all acclaim

     G   D7   G7
That wondrous, glorious name of Je - sus.

Chorus 2   *Repeat Chorus 1*

Verse 3

      C   Cdim7 C F   C G7/F C/E
And someday I   shall see Him face to   face

C   Cdim7 C F   G7   C
To thank and praise   Him for His won - drous grace,

G7   Em/G G7 Em/G G7
Which He   gave to   me

C F   C
When He made me free,

     G   D7   G7
The blessed Son of God called Je - sus.

Chorus 3   *Repeat Chorus 1*

Jesus Paid It All

Words by Elvina M. Hall
Music by John T. Grape

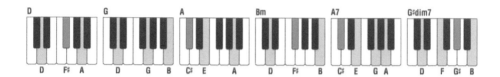

Verse 1

    D G/D D
I hear the Savior say,

  D/F♯ A   **Bm A D**
"Thy strength in - deed is small.

       G/D D
Child of weak - ness, watch and pray,

D/F♯ G D/A   **A7 D**
Find   in Me thine all in all."

Chorus 1

  G/D D
Je - sus paid it all,

  G/D D   **A**
All to Him I owe.

D G/D D   **D/F♯ G**
Sin had left a crim - son   stain,

G♯°7 D/A   **A7 D**
He   washed it white as snow.

PIANO CHORD SONGBOOK

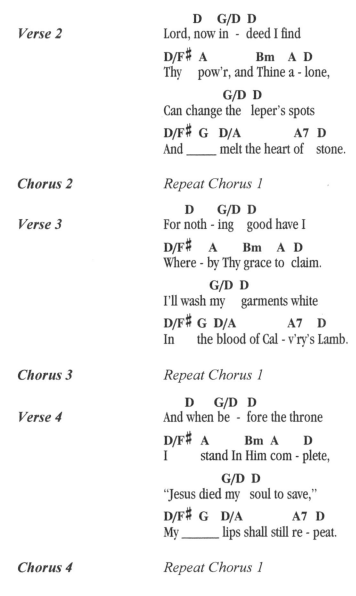

Verse 2

    D   **G/D D**
Lord, now in - deed I find

D/F♯ A   **Bm A D**
Thy   pow'r, and Thine a - lone,

      G/D D
Can change the leper's spots

D/F♯ G D/A   **A7 D**
And _____ melt the heart of   stone.

Chorus 2   *Repeat Chorus 1*

Verse 3

    D   **G/D D**
For noth - ing   good have I

D/F♯   **A**   **Bm A D**
Where - by Thy grace to claim.

      G/D D
I'll wash my   garments white

D/F♯ G D/A   **A7   D**
In   the blood of Cal - v'ry's Lamb.

Chorus 3   *Repeat Chorus 1*

Verse 4

    D   **G/D D**
And when be - fore the throne

D/F♯ A   **Bm A**   **D**
I   stand In Him com - plete,

      G/D D
"Jesus died my   soul to save,"

D/F♯ G D/A   **A7 D**
My _____ lips shall still re - peat.

Chorus 4   *Repeat Chorus 1*

Just a Closer Walk with Thee

Traditional
Arranged by Kenneth Morris

Melody:

I am weak but Thou art strong.

Bb   Bbdim7   Cm7   F7

Eb   Bb7   Edim7

Verse 1

Bb   Bbdim7 Cm7   F7
I am weak but Thou art   strong.

           Eb/F   Bb
Jesus, keep me from all wrong.

       Bb7   Eb Edim7
I'll be satisfied as long

      Bb   F7   Bb
As I walk, let me walk close to Thee.

Chorus 1

Bb   Bbdim7 Cm7   F7
Just a closer walk with   Thee,

           Eb/F Bb
Grant it, Jesus, is my plea.

       Bb7   Eb Edim7
Daily walking close to Thee,

      Bb   F7   Bb
Let it be, dear Lord, let it be.

Verse 2

Bb   Bbdim7 Cm7   F7
Through this world of toil and   snares,

         Eb/F   Bb
If I falter, Lord, who cares?

        Bb7   Eb   Edim7
Who with me my burden shares?

        Bb   F7   Bb
None but Thee, dear Lord, none but Thee.

Chorus 2   *Repeat Chorus 1*

Verse 3

Bb   Bbdim7 Cm7 F7
When my feeble life is   o'er,

         Eb/F Bb
Time for me will be no more.

        Bb7   Eb   Edim7
Guide me gently, safely o'er

        Bb   F7   Bb
To Thy kingdom shore, to Thy shore.

Chorus 3   *Repeat Chorus 1*

Just As I Am

Words by Charlotte Elliott
Music by William B. Bradbury

Just _ as I am, __ with - out __ one plea,

Verse 1

  Eb   Bb   Eb
Just as I am, with - out one plea,

  Bb Eb/Bb Bb7   Ab/Eb Eb
But that Thy   blood was shed for me,

                Ab
And that Thou bidd'st me come to Thee,

  Eb   Bb   Eb
O Lamb of God, I come! I come!

Verse 2

  Eb   Bb   Eb
Just as I am, and waiting not

  Bb Eb/Bb Bb7   Ab/Eb Eb
To rid my   soul of one   dark blot,

                 Ab
To Thee whose blood can cleanse each spot,

  Eb   Bb   Eb
O Lamb of God, I come! I come!

Verse 3

Eb   Bb   Eb
Just as I am, though tossed a - bout

Bb   Eb/Bb Bb7   Ab/Eb Eb
With many a   conflict, many a doubt.

Ab
Fighting and fears with - in, without,

Eb   Bb   Eb
O Lamb of God, I come! I come!

Verse 4

Eb   Bb   Eb
Just as I am, poor, wretched, blind;

Bb   Eb/Bb Bb7   Ab/Eb Eb
Sight, rich - es, healing of   the mind —

Ab
Yea, all I need in Thee to find,

Eb   Bb   Eb
O Lamb of God, I come! I come!

Verse 5

Eb   Bb   Eb
Just as I am, Thou wilt re - ceive,

Bb   Eb/Bb Bb7   Ab/Eb Eb
Wilt wel - come, pardon, cleanse, relieve.

Ab
Because Thy promise I believe,

Eb   Bb   Eb
O Lamb of God, I come! I come!

Verse 6

Eb   Bb   Eb
Just as I am, Thy love un - known

Bb   Eb/Bb Bb7 Ab/Eb Eb
Hath bro - ken ev'ry bar - rier down.

Ab
Now to be Thine, yea, Thine alone,

Eb   Bb   Eb
O Lamb of God, I come! I come!

Just Over in the Gloryland

Words by James W. Acuff
Music by Emmett S. Dean

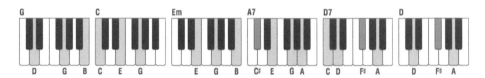

Verse 1

       G   C/G G   C   C/E G
I've a home pre - pared where the saints a - bide,

   Em   A7   D7
Just over in the glory - land.

       G   C/G G   C   C/E G
And I long to   be by my Sav - ior's side,

   Em   G/D D7 G
Just over in the glo - ry - land.

Chorus 1

       G   D7 G
Just over in the gloryland

G/B C   C/E G
I'll   join the happy an - gel band,

   Em   A7   D   A7
Just over in the glory - land.

D   G   D7 G
  Just over in the gloryland,

G/B C   G
There with the mighty host I'll stand,

   Em   G/D D7 G C/G G
Just over in the glo - ry - land.

Verse 2

    G C/G G   C   C/E G
I am on my   way to those man - sions fair,

   Em   A7   D7
Just over in the glory - land.

     G C/G G   C C/E G
There to sing God's praise and His glo - ry   share,

   Em   G/D D7 G
Just over in the glo - ry - land.

Chorus 2   *Repeat Chorus 1*

Verse 3

     G C/G G   C   C/E G
What a joy - ful   thought that my Lord I'll   see,

   Em   A7   D7
Just over in the glory - land.

     G   C/G G   C C/E G
And with kin - dred saved, there for - ev - er   be,

   Em   G/D D7 G
Just over in the glo - ry - land.

Chorus 3   *Repeat Chorus 1*

Verse 4

     G   C/G   G   C   C/E G
With the blood - washed throng I will shout and sing,

   Em   A7   D7
Just over in the glory - land.

     G   C/G G   C   C/E G
Glad ho - san - nas to Christ, the Lord and King,

   Em   G/D D7 G
Just over in the glo - ry - land.

Chorus 4   *Repeat Chorus 1*

Leaning on the Everlasting Arms

Words by Elisha A. Hoffman
Music by Anthony J. Showalter

Verse 1

A♭   D♭6 D♭
What a fellowship, what a joy divine,

A♭   B♭7 E♭7
Leaning on the Ever - lasting Arms!

A♭   D♭6   D♭
What a blessedness, what a peace is mine,

A♭   E♭7 A♭
Leaning on the Everlast - ing Arms!

Chorus 1

A♭ D♭ A♭   B♭7 E♭
Leaning, leaning, safe and secure from all a - larms.

A♭ D♭ A♭   E♭7 A♭
Leaning, leaning, leaning on the Everlast - ing Arms!

Verse 2

Ab   Db6   Db
O how sweet to walk in this pilgrim way,

Ab   Bb7   Eb7
Leaning on the Ever - lasting Arms!

Ab   Db6   Db
O how bright the path grows from day to day,

Ab   Eb7 Ab
Leaning on the Everlast - ing Arms!

Chorus 2   *Repeat Chorus 1*

Verse 3

Ab   Db6   Db
What have I to dread, what have I to fear,

Ab   Bb7   Eb7
Leaning on the Ever - lasting Arms?

Ab   Db6   Db
I have blessed peace with my Lord so near,

Ab   Eb7 Ab
Leaning on the Everlast - ing Arms!

Chorus 3   *Repeat Chorus 1*

The Lily of the Valley

Words by Charles W. Fry
Music by William S. Hays

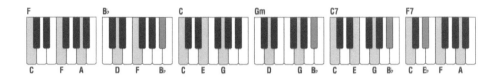

I have found a friend in Je - sus, He's...

F   Bb   C   Gm   C7   F7

Verse 1

      F   Bb   F   Bb   F
I have found a friend in Jesus, He's ev'rything to me.

                Bb   F/A   F   C
He's the fairest of ten thou - sand to my soul.

    F   Bb F   Bb   F
The Lily of   the Valley, in Him alone I see,

               Gm/Bb   F   C7   F
All I need to cleanse and make me ful - ly   whole.

F7/A   Bb   F
In   sorrow He's my comfort, in trou - ble He's my stay,

         Bb   F/A   F   C
He tells me ev'ry care on Him to   roll.

Chorus 1

        F   Bb F
He's the Lily of   the Valley,

   Bb   F
The Bright and Morning Star.

           Gm/Bb   F   C7   F
He's the fairest of ten thousand to   my   soul.

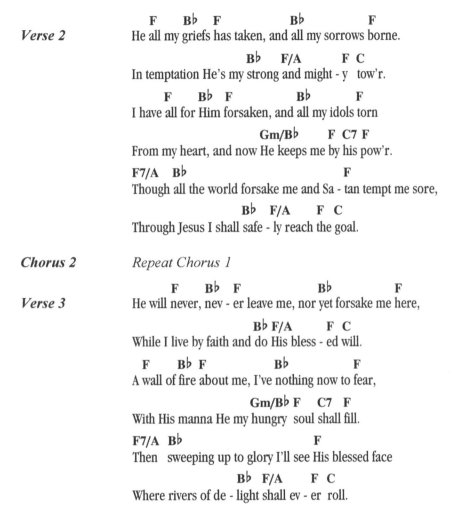

Verse 2

      F   B♭ F   B♭   F

He all my griefs has taken, and all my sorrows borne.

                         B♭   F/A   F C

In temptation He's my strong and might - y tow'r.

      F   B♭ F   B♭   F

I have all for Him forsaken, and all my idols torn

                      Gm/B♭   F C7 F

From my heart, and now He keeps me by his pow'r.

F7/A B♭   F

Though all the world forsake me and Sa - tan tempt me sore,

                 B♭ F/A   F C

Through Jesus I shall safe - ly reach the goal.

Chorus 2   *Repeat Chorus 1*

               F   B♭ F   B♭   F

Verse 3   He will never, nev - er leave me, nor yet forsake me here,

                     B♭ F/A   F C

While I live by faith and do His bless - ed will.

      F   B♭ F   B♭   F

A wall of fire about me, I've nothing now to fear,

                   Gm/B♭ F   C7 F

With His manna He my hungry soul shall fill.

F7/A B♭   F

Then   sweeping up to glory I'll see His blessed face

                 B♭ F/A   F C

Where rivers of de - light shall ev - er roll.

Chorus 3   *Repeat Chorus 1*

Little Is Much When God Is in It

Words by Mrs. F.W. Suffield
and Dwight Brock
Music by Mrs. F.W. Suffield

In the har - vest field now rip - ened,

Verse 1

      D
In the harvest field now ripened,

G   **D**   **E7**   **A**
There is work for all to do.

A7   **D**
Hark, the voice of God is calling,

G   **D**   **A7 D**
To the harvest call - ing you.

Chorus 1

    D   **G/D D**
Little is much when God is in it.

       G/D D   **A**
Labor not for   wealth or fame.

A7   **D**
There's a crown, and you can win it

G   **D**   **A7 D**
If you go in Je - sus' name.

Verse 2

D
Does the place you're called to labor

G   D   E7   A
Seem so small and little - known?

A7 D
It is great if God is in it,

G   D   A7 D
And He'll not forget His own.

Chorus 2   *Repeat Chorus 1*

Verse 3

D
Are you laid aside from service,

G   D   E7   A
Body worn from toil and care?

A7   D
You can still be in the battle

G   D   A7 D
In the sacred place of   prayer.

Chorus 3   *Repeat Chorus 1*

Verse 4

D
When the conflict here is ended

G   D   E7   A
And our race on earth is run,

A7   D
He will say, if we are faithful,

G   D   A7   D
"Welcome home, my child, well done."

Chorus 4   *Repeat Chorus 1*

Love Lifted Me

Words by James Rowe
Music by Howard E. Smith

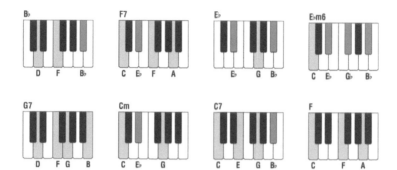

Verse 1

     B♭   F7
I was sinking deep in sin, far from the peaceful shore,

                        B♭
Very deeply stained within, sinking to rise no more.

                           E♭
But the Master of the sea heard my despairing cry,

     E♭m6 B♭   E♭ B♭ F7 B♭
From the wa - ters   lifted me, now safe am I.

Chorus 1

     F7   B♭ E♭/B♭ B♭   E♭ G7/D Cm
Love lifted me! _____ Love lifted me!

E♭   B♭   C7   F F7
When nothing else could help, love lifted me.

B♭ F7 B♭ E♭/B♭ B♭   E♭ G7/D Cm
Love lifted me! _____ Love lifted me!

E♭   B♭   F7 B♭
When nothing else could help, love lift - ed me.

Verse 2

Bb   F7
All my heart to Him I give, ever to Him I'll cling,

                                          Bb
In His blessed presence live, ever His praises sing.

                                          Eb
Love so mighty and so true merits my soul's best songs;

Ebm6 Bb   Eb Bb F7 Bb
Faithful lov - ing   service, too, to Him be - longs.

Chorus 2   *Repeat Chorus 1*

Bb   F7
Verse 3   Souls in danger, look above, Jesus completely saves.

                                          Bb
He will lift you, by His love, out of the angry waves.

                                          Eb
He's the Master of the sea, billows His will o - bey.

Ebm6 Bb   Eb Bb   F7 Bb
He your Sav - ior   wants to be; be saved to - day.

Chorus 3   *Repeat Chorus 1*

The Love of God

Words and Music by
Frederick M. Lehman

Verse 1

      D   A   D
The love of God is greater far than tongue or pen can ever tell.

                              A7   D
It goes beyond the highest star, and reaches to the lowest hell.

    G   D   A A7 D
The guilty pair, bowed down with care, God gave His Son to win.

    G   D   A7   D
His erring child He recon - ciled, and pardoned from his sin.

Chorus 1

D   G   D
O love of God, how rich and pure!

         A   D
How measure - less and strong!

       G   D
It shall for - evermore en - dure –

       A7   D
The saints' and angels' song.

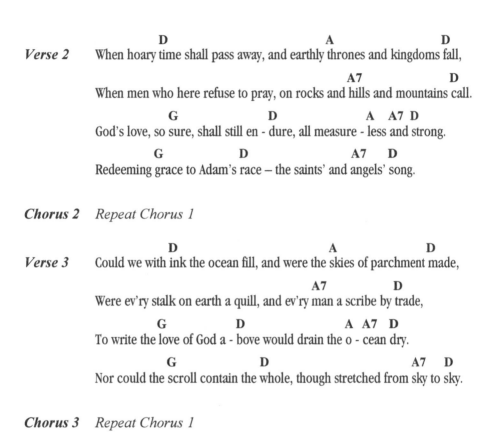

Verse 2 When hoary time shall pass away, and earthly thrones and kingdoms fall,
            D   A   D

                                        A7   D
          When men who here refuse to pray, on rocks and hills and mountains call.
          G   D   A A7 D
          God's love, so sure, shall still en - dure, all measure - less and strong.
          G   D   A7   D
          Redeeming grace to Adam's race – the saints' and angels' song.

Chorus 2 *Repeat Chorus 1*

Verse 3 Could we with ink the ocean fill, and were the skies of parchment made,
          D   A   D

                                        A7   D
          Were ev'ry stalk on earth a quill, and ev'ry man a scribe by trade,
          G   D   A A7 D
          To write the love of God a - bove would drain the o - cean dry.
          G   D   A7   D
          Nor could the scroll contain the whole, though stretched from sky to sky.

Chorus 3 *Repeat Chorus 1*

My Savior First of All

Words by Fanny J. Crosby
Music by John R. Sweney

Melody:

When my life-work is end-ed and I cross the swell-ing tide,

Verse 1

           G   **C**   **G**
When my lifework is ended and I cross the swelling tide,

                   D/F♯ A7/E D
When the bright and glorious morning I   shall   see,

G   **G/B** **C**
I shall know my Redeemer when I reach the other side,

       G   **D7** **C/D D7** **G**
And His smile will be the first to wel - come me.

Chorus 1

       D7   **C/D D7** **G**
I shall know Him, I   shall know Him,

              D7/A G D/F♯ A7/E D
And redeemed by His side _____ I   shall stand.

G/D D7 G   **C/G G C**
I   shall know Him, I   shall know Him

      G   **D** **C/D D7 G**
By the prints of the nails in   His hand.

Verse 2

G   C   G
O the soul-thrilling rapture when I view His blessed face,

                       D/F♯ A7/E D
And the luster of His kindly beam - ing   eye.

G   G/B   C
How my full heart will praise Him for the mercy, love, and grace

                  G   D7   C/D D7 G
That pre - pare for me a mansion in   the sky.

Chorus 2   *Repeat Chorus 1*

Verse 3

                  G   C   G
O the dear ones in glory, how they beckon me to come,

                       D/F♯ A7/E D
And our parting at the river I   re - call.

G   G/B   C
To the sweet vales of Eden they will sing my welcome home,

             G   D7   C/D D7 G
But I long to meet my Savior first of all.

Chorus 3   *Repeat Chorus 1*

Verse 4

                  G   C   G
Through the gates to the city, in a robe of spotless white,

                        D/F♯ A7/E D
He will lead me where no tears will ev - er   fall.

G   G/B   C
In the glad song of ages I shall mingle with delight,

             G   D7   C/D D7 G
But I long to meet my Savior first of all.

Chorus 4   *Repeat Chorus 1*

Near the Cross

Words by Fanny Crosby
Music by William H. Doane

Verse 1

F   Dm B♭
Jesus, keep me near the cross,

F   C
There a precious fountain,

F   Dm B♭
Free to all, a healing stream,

F   C7 F
Flows from Calv'ry's moun - tain.

Chorus 1

F   B♭
In the cross, in the cross

F B♭ C
Be my glory ever,

F   Dm B♭
Till my raptured soul shall find

F   C7 F
Rest beyond the riv - er.

Verse 2

F   Dm   B♭
Near the cross, a trembling soul,

F   C
Love and mercy found me.

F   Dm   B♭
There the Bright and Morning Star

F   C7   F
Sheds its beams a - round me.

Chorus 2

Repeat Chorus 1

Verse 3

F   Dm   B♭
Near the cross! Oh, Lamb of God,

F   C
Bring its scenes be - fore me.

F   Dm   B♭
Help me walk from day to day

F   C7   F
With its shadow o'er me.

Chorus 3

Repeat Chorus 1

Verse 4

F   Dm   B♭
Near the cross! I'll watch and wait,

F   C
Hoping, trusting ever,

F   Dm   B♭
Till I reach the golden strand,

F   C7   F
Just beyond the riv - er.

Chorus 4

Repeat Chorus 1

A New Name in Glory

Words and Music by
C. Austin Miles

Melody:

I was once a sin-ner, but I came,

G   D   D7   A7

Verse 1

> **G**   **C/G G G/B D G**
> I was once a sin - ner, but I came,
>
> **D7**   **G**
> Pardon to receive from my Lord.
>
>   **C/G G G/B D G**
> This was freely giv - en, and I found
>
> **A7**   **D7**
> That He always kept His word.

Chorus 1

>   **G**
> There's a new name written down in glory,
>
>   **C**   **G**
> And it's mine, O yes, it's mine.
>
>   **D7**   **G**
> And the white robed angels sing the story,
>
> **A7**   **D7**
> "A sinner has come home."
>
>   **G**
> For there's a new name written down in glory,
>
>   **C**   **G**
> And it's mine, O yes, it's mine.
>
>   **C**   **G**   **C**
> With my sins forgiven I am bound for heav - en,
>
> **G**   **D7**   **G**
> Never - more to roam.

Verse 2

G   C/G G G/B D G
I was humbly kneel - ing at the cross,

D7   G
Fearing naught but God's angry frown,

        C/G G   G/B D G
When the heavens o - pened and I saw

A7   D7
That my name was written down.

Chorus 2   *Repeat Chorus 1*

Verse 3

G   C/G G G/B D G
In the Book 'tis writ - ten, "Saved by grace."

D7   G
O the joy that came to my soul.

        C/G G G/B D G
Now I am for - giv - en, and I know

A7   D7
By the blood I am made whole.

Chorus 3   *Repeat Chorus 1*

No, Not One!

Words by Johnson Oatman, Jr.
Music by George C. Hugg

Melody:

There's not a friend like the low - ly Je - sus,

F
C F A

B♭
D F B♭

C
C E G

C7
C E G B♭

Verse 1

     F   F/A B♭   F
There's not a friend like the lowly Je - sus,

       C   F C7 F
No, not one! No, not one!

            F/A B♭   F
None else could heal all our soul's diseas - es,

       C   F C7 F
No, not one! No, not one!

Chorus 1

F   C7   F
Jesus knows all about our strug - gles;

               C
He will guide till the day is done.

F   F/A B♭   F
There's not a friend like the lowly Je - sus,

     C   F C7 F
No, not one! No, not one!

Verse 2

F   F/A B♭   F
No friend like Him is so high and ho - ly,

     C   F C7 F
No, not one! No, not one!

           F/A B♭   F
And yet no friend is so meek and low - ly,

     C   F C7 F
No, not one! No, not one!

Chorus 2   *Repeat Chorus 1*

Verse 3

```
F                 F/A  B♭      F
```
There's not an hour that He is not near us,

```
    C   F  C7 F
```
No, not one! No, not one!

```
              F/A   B♭          F
```
No night so dark but His love can cheer us,

```
    C   F  C7 F
```
No, not one! No, not one!

Chorus 3   *Repeat Chorus 1*

Verse 4

```
F            F/A   B♭           F
```
Did ever saint find this friend forsake him?

```
    C   F  C7 F
```
No, not one! No, not one!

```
          F/A   B♭          F
```
Or sinner find that He would not take him?

```
    C   F  C7 F
```
No, not one! No, not one!

Chorus 4   *Repeat Chorus 1*

Verse 5

```
F          F/A        B♭      F
```
Was e'er a gift like the Savior giv - en?

```
    C   F  C7 F
```
No, not one! No, not one!

```
          F/A  B♭          F
```
Will He refuse us a home in heav - en?

```
    C   F  C7 F
```
No, not one! No, not one!

Chorus 5   *Repeat Chorus 1*

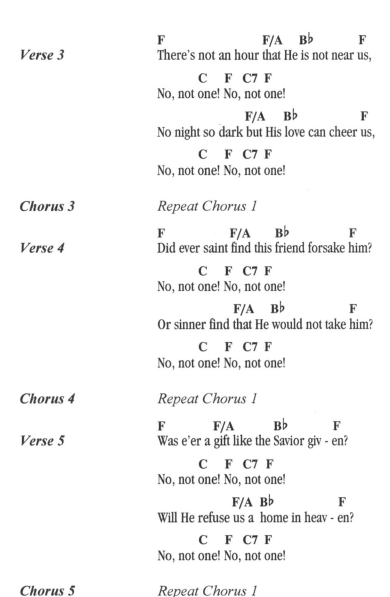

Nothing But the Blood

Words and Music by
Robert Lowry

Melody:

What can wash a - way my sin?

Verse 1

       G   D G
What can wash a - way my sin?

                D7 G
Nothing but the blood of Je - sus.

             D G
What can make me whole again?

                D7 G
Nothing but the blood of Je - sus.

Chorus 1

       G   D   G
Oh, pre - cious is the flow

D7   G/D D   G
That makes me   white as snow.

            D G
No oth - er fount I know,

                D7 G
Nothing but the blood of Je - sus.

PIANO CHORD SONGBOOK

Verse 2

G　　　D　G
For my par - don this I see,

　　　　　　D7　G
Nothing but the blood of Je - sus.

　　　　　　D　G
For my cleans - ing, this my plea,

　　　　　　D7　G
Nothing but the blood of Je - sus.

Chorus 2　　　　　*Repeat Chorus 1*

Verse 3

G　　　D　G
Nothing can for sin atone,

　　　　　　D7　G
Nothing but the blood of Je - sus.

　　　　　　D　G
Naught of good that I have done,

　　　　　　D7　G
Nothing but the blood of Je - sus.

Chorus 3　　　　　*Repeat Chorus 1*

Verse 4

G　　　D　G
This is all my hope and peace,

　　　　　　D7　G
Nothing but the blood of Je - sus.

　　　　　　D　G
This is all my righteousness,

　　　　　　D7　G
Nothing but the blood of Je - sus.

Chorus 4　　　　　*Repeat Chorus 1*

Oh, How I Love Jesus

Words by Frederick Whitfield
Traditional American Melody

Melody:

There is a name I love to hear,

Verse 1
$\quad$ G $\qquad\qquad$ D $\qquad$ G
There is a name I love to hear, I love to sing its worth.
$\qquad\qquad\qquad\qquad\qquad$ C $\quad$ G/D D7 G
It sounds like music in my ear, the sweetest name on earth.

Chorus 1
$\quad$ G $\qquad$ D7 $\qquad$ G
Oh, how I love Jesus! Oh, how I love Jesus!
$\qquad\qquad\qquad\qquad$ C $\quad$ G/D D7 $\quad$ G
Oh, how I love Jesus, be - cause he first loved me.

Verse 2
$\quad$ G $\qquad\qquad$ D $\qquad$ G
It tells me of a Savior's love, who died to set me free.
$\qquad\qquad\qquad\qquad\qquad$ C $\quad$ G/D D7 G
It tells me of His precious blood, the sinner's per - fect plea.

Chorus 2 $\qquad$ *Repeat Chorus 1*

Verse 3
$\quad$ G $\qquad\qquad$ D $\qquad$ G
It tells me what my Father hath in store for ev'ry day,
$\qquad\qquad\qquad\qquad\qquad$ C $\quad$ G/D D7 G
And though I tread a darksome path, yields sunshine all $\quad$ the way.

Chorus 3 $\qquad$ *Repeat Chorus 1*

Verse 4
$\quad$ G $\qquad\qquad$ D $\qquad$ G
It tells of One whose loving heart can feel my deepest woe,
$\qquad\qquad\qquad\qquad$ C $\quad$ G/D D7 $\quad$ G
Who in each sorrow bears a part, that none can bear be - low.

Chorus 4 $\qquad$ *Repeat Chorus 1*

Revive Us Again

Words by William P. MacKay
Music by John J. Husband

Melody:

We praise Thee, O God, for the Son of Thy love,

F   B♭   C   C7

C   F   A   D   F   B♭   C   E   G   C   E   G   B♭

Verse 1

     F
We praise Thee, O God, for the Son of Thy love,
     B♭   F   C
For Jesus, who died and is now gone above.

Chorus 1

    F   B♭ F
Halle - lu - jah! Thine the glory!
    B♭   F   C
Halle - lu - jah! A - men!
    F   B♭ F
Halle - lu - jah! Thine the glory!
     B♭   F C7 F
Re - vive us a - gain.

Verse 2

     F
We praise Thee, O God, for Thy Spirit of Light,
     B♭   F   C
Who has shown us our Sav - ior and scat - tered our night.

Chorus 2   *Repeat Chorus 1*

Verse 3

     F
All glory and praise to the Lamb that was slain,
     B♭   F   C
Who has borne all our sins and has cleansed ev'ry stain.

Chorus 3   *Repeat Chorus 1*

Verse 4

     F
Re - vive us again, fill each heart with Thy love.
     B♭   F   C
May each soul be re - kin - dled with fire from above.

Chorus 4   *Repeat Chorus 1*

The Old Rugged Cross

Words and Music by
Rev. George Bennard

Melody:

On a hill far a-way stood an old rug-ged cross,

Verse 1

Bb   Eb
On a hill far away stood an old rugged cross,

C   F7   Bb
The emblem of suff'ring and shame.

                      Eb
And I love that old cross, where the dearest and best

C   F7   Bb
For a world of lost sinners was slain.

Chorus 1

     F7   Bb
So I'll cherish the old rugged cross,

    Eb   Bb
Till my trophies at last I lay down.

                Eb
I will cling to the old rugged cross,

     Bb   F7   Bb
And ex - change it some - day for a crown.

Verse 2

Bb   Eb
Oh, that old rugged cross, so de - spised by the world,

C   F7   Bb
Has a wondrous attraction for me.

                           Eb
For the dear Lamb of God left His glory above

C F7   Bb
To bear it to dark Calva - ry.

Chorus 2   *Repeat Chorus 1*

Verse 3

Bb   Eb
In the old rugged cross, stained with blood so divine,

C F7   Bb
A wondrous beauty I see.

                        Eb
For 'twas on that old cross Jesus suffered and died

C F7   Bb
To pardon and sanctify me.

Chorus 3   *Repeat Chorus 1*

Verse 4

Bb   Eb
To the old rugged cross I will ever be true,

C F7   Bb
Its shame and reproach gladly bear.

                      Eb
Then He'll call me someday to my home far away,

C   F7   Bb
Where His glory forever I'll share.

Chorus 4   *Repeat Chorus 1*

On Jordan's Stormy Banks

Words by Samuel Stennett
Traditional American Melody
Arranged by Rigdon M. McIntosh

Verse 1

   D   A7
On Jordan's stormy banks I stand,

   D   A
And cast a wishful eye

A7 D
To Canaan's fair and happy land,

    G D A7 D
Where ___ my pos - sessions lie.

Chorus 1

   D   A7
I am bound for the Promised Land,

   D   A
I am bound for the Promised Land.

A7 D
O who will come and go with me?

 G D   A7   D
I am bound for the Promised Land.

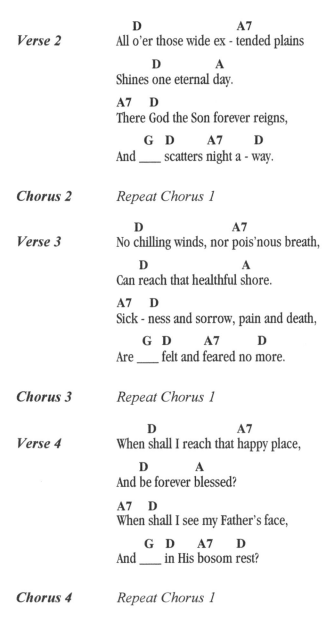

Verse 2

> D   A7
> All o'er those wide ex - tended plains
>
>   D   A
> Shines one eternal day.
>
> A7 D
> There God the Son forever reigns,
>
>   G D   A7   D
> And ___ scatters night a - way.

Chorus 2   *Repeat Chorus 1*

Verse 3

> D   A7
> No chilling winds, nor pois'nous breath,
>
>   D   A
> Can reach that healthful shore.
>
> A7 D
> Sick - ness and sorrow, pain and death,
>
>   G D   A7   D
> Are ___ felt and feared no more.

Chorus 3   *Repeat Chorus 1*

Verse 4

>   D   A7
> When shall I reach that happy place,
>
>   D   A
> And be forever blessed?
>
> A7 D
> When shall I see my Father's face,
>
>   G D A7   D
> And ___ in His bosom rest?

Chorus 4   *Repeat Chorus 1*

Pass Me Not, O Gentle Savior

Words by Fanny J. Crosby
Music by William H. Doane

Pass me not, O gen - tle Sav - ior,

Verse 1

G G/B C   G G/B
Pass me   not, O gentle Sav - ior,

D   G/B   D G
Hear my hum - ble cry.

     G/B C   G G/B
While on   others Thou art call - ing,

D7   G/D D7 G
Do not pass me by.

Chorus 1

G   C   G   G/B D
Savior, Savior, hear my hum - ble cry.

G G/B C   G   G/B
While on   others Thou art call - ing,

D7   G/D D7 G
Do not pass me by.

Verse 2

```
G  G/B C              G    G/B
Let me   at the throne of mer - cy

D    G/B  D   G
Find a sweet re - lief.

      G/B C                 G   G/B
Kneel - ing  there in deep con - tri - tion,

D7      G/D  D7  G
Help my un  -  be - lief.
```

Chorus 2   *Repeat Chorus 1*

Verse 3

```
G    G/B C              G    G/B
Trust - ing  only in Thy mer - it,

D      G/B D  G
Would I seek Thy face.

     G/B  C                G   G/B
Heal my   wounded, broken spir - it,

D7      G/D D7  G
Save me by    Thy grace.
```

Chorus 3   *Repeat Chorus 1*

Verse 4

```
G   G/B  C                G    G/B
Thou, the  Spring of all my com - fort,

D        G/B D  G
More than life  to  me,

     G/B C                G   G/B
Whom have I on earth be - side Thee?

D7      G/D   D7  G
Whom in heav'n but Thee?
```

Chorus 4   *Repeat Chorus 1*

Precious Memories

Words and Music by
J.B.F. Wright

Pre - cious mem -'ries,   un - seen an - gels,

A♭	D♭	E♭7	Fm	B♭7
C E♭ A♭	D♭ F A♭	D♭ E♭ G B♭	C F A♭	D F A♭ B♭

Verse 1

      A♭   **D♭**   **A♭**
Precious mem'ries, unseen an - gels,

       E♭7 Fm   **B♭7 E♭7**
Sent from somewhere to my soul.

      A♭   **D♭**   **A♭**
How they linger, ever near me,

       A♭/C E♭7 Fm A♭ E♭7 A♭
And the   sa - cred past un - fold.

Chorus 1

      A♭
Precious mem'ries, how they linger,

      D♭   **A♭**
How they ever flood my soul.

            D♭   **A♭**
In the stillness of the mid - night,

      A♭/C E♭7 Fm A♭   **E♭7 A♭**
Pre - cious sa - cred scenes un - fold.

Verse 2

Ab   Db   Ab
Precious father, loving moth - er,

  Eb7 Fm   Bb7   Eb7
Fly a - cross the lonely years;

Ab   Db   Ab
And old home scenes of my child - hood

  Ab/C Eb7 Fm Ab Eb7 Ab
In fond   mem - o - ry ap - pear.

Chorus 2   *Repeat Chorus 1*

Verse 3

Ab   Db   Ab
As I travel on life's path - way,

  Eb7 Fm   Bb7   Eb7
Know not what the years may hold.

Ab   Db   Ab
As I ponder, hope grows fon - der,

  Ab/C Eb7   Fm Ab Eb7 Ab
Pre - cious mem - 'ries flood my soul.

Chorus 3   *Repeat Chorus 1*

Rock of Ages

Words by Augustus M. Toplady
V.1,2,4 altered by Thomas Cotterill
Music by Thomas Hastings

Rock of Ag - es, cleft for me,

Bb   Eb   Bb   Eb6   F7

D F Bb   Eb G Bb   C Eb G Bb   C Eb F A

Verse 1

    Bb   Eb   Bb
Rock of Ages, cleft for me,

Bb/D Eb6 Bb   F7 Bb
Let   me hide myself in Thee.

      F7   Bb
Let the water and the blood

       F7   Bb
From Thy wounded side which flowed,

   Eb Bb   Eb   Bb
Be of sin the double cure,

Bb/D Eb6 Bb   F7 Bb
Save   from wrath and make me pure.

Verse 2

     Bb   Eb Bb
Could my tears for - ever flow,

Bb/D Eb6 Bb   F7 Bb
Could my zeal no lan - guor know,

      F7   Bb
These for sin could not a - tone,

      F7   Bb
Thou must save, and Thou a - lone.

  Eb Bb   Eb   Bb
In my hand no price I bring,

Bb/D Eb6 Bb   F7 Bb
Sim - ply to Thy cross I   cling.

Verse 3

Bb   Eb   Bb
Nothing in my hand I bring,

Bb/D Eb6 Bb   F7 Bb
Sim - ply   to Thy cross I   cling.

F7   Bb
Naked, come to Thee for dress,

F7   Bb
Helpless, look to Thee for grace.

Eb Bb   Eb   Bb
Foul, I   to the fountain fly,

Bb/D Eb6 Bb   F7 Bb
Wash me, Savior, or I   die.

Verse 4

Bb   Eb   Bb
While I draw this fleeting breath,

Bb/D Eb6 Bb   F7 Bb
When my eyes shall close in death,

F7   Bb
When I rise to worlds un - known

F7   Bb
And be - hold Thee on Thy throne,

Eb Bb   Eb   Bb
Rock of Ages, cleft for me,

Bb/D Eb6 Bb   F7 Bb
Let   me hide myself in Thee.

Send the Light

Words and Music by
Charles H. Gabriel

Verse 1

        G
There's a call comes ringing o'er the restless wave,

        D7   **G**
"Send the light! Send the light!"

There are souls to rescue, there are souls to save.

        D7   **G**
Send the light! Send the light!

Chorus 1

        G
Send the light, the blessed gospel light.

D7   **G**
Let it shine from shore to shore.

Send the light, the blessed gospel light,

D7   **G**
Let it shine forever - more.

| | **G** |
| *Verse 2* | We have heard the Macedonian call today, |

        D7   **G**
"Send the light! Send the light!"

And a golden off'ring at the cross we lay.
        D7   **G**
Send the light! Send the light!

Chorus 2   *Repeat Chorus 1*

        G
Verse 3   Let us pray that grace may ev'rywhere abound,

        D7   **G**
"Send the light! Send the light!"

And a Christ-like Spirit ev'rywhere be found.
        D7   **G**
Send the light! Send the light!

Chorus 3   *Repeat Chorus 1*

        G
Verse 4   Let us not grow weary in the work of love,

        D7   **G**
"Send the light! Send the light!"

Let us gather jewels for a crown above.
        D7   **G**
Send the light! Send the light!

Chorus 4   *Repeat Chorus 1*

Shall We Gather at the River?

Words and Music by
Robert Lowry

Verse 1

D   A7
Shall we gather at the river, where bright angel feet have trod,

D   A   A7   D
With its crystal tide forever flowing by the throne of God?

Chorus 1

G   D
Yes, we'll gather at the river,

  A7   D
The beautiful, the beautiful river.

G   D
Gather with the saints at the river

  A   A7   D
That flows by the throne of God.

Verse 2

D   A7
On the bosom of the river, where the Savior King we own,

D   A   A7   D
We shall meet, and sorrow never 'neath the glory of the throne.

Chorus 2   *Repeat Chorus 1*

Verse 3

D   A7
Ere we reach the shining river, lay we ev'ry burden down.

D   A   A7   D
Grace our spirits will deliver and pro - vide a robe and crown.

Chorus 3   *Repeat Chorus 1*

Verse 4

D   A7
Soon we'll reach the shining river, soon our pilgrimage will cease.

D   A   A7   D
Soon our happy hearts will quiver with the melo - dy of peace.

Chorus 4   *Repeat Chorus 1*

There Is a Balm in Gilead

African-American Spiritual

Chorus 1

    F   Bb   F C7
There is a balm in Gilead to make the wound - ed whole.

    F   C7   F
There is a balm in Gilead to heal the sin - sick soul.

Verse 1

    F   Bb   F   C7
Sometimes I feel dis - couraged, and think my works in vain,

      F   Bb   F   C7   Dm Bb
But then the Holy Spirit re - vives my soul a - gain.

Chorus 2   *Repeat Chorus 1*

Verse 2

    F   Bb   F   C7
Don't ever feel dis - couraged, for Jesus is your friend.

      F   Bb   F   C7   Dm Bb
And if you lack for knowledge, He'll not re - fuse to lend.

Chorus 3   *Repeat Chorus 1*

Verse 3

    F   Bb   F   C7
If you cannot preach like Peter, if you cannot pray like Paul,

      F   Bb   F   C7   Dm Bb
You can tell the love of Jesus and say, "He died for all."

Chorus 4   *Repeat Chorus 1*

Since Jesus Came Into My Heart

Words by Rufus H. McDaniel
Music by Charles H. Gabriel

Melody:

What a won-der-ful change in my life has been wrought

Verse 1

       Ab
What a wonderful change in my life has been wrought

   Db   Ab
Since Jesus came into my heart.

I have light in my soul for which long I had sought,

   Bb7   Eb Ab Eb7
Since Jesus came into my heart.

Chorus 1

   Ab
Since Jesus came into my heart,

   Db   Ab
Since Jesus came into my heart;

Floods of joy o'er my soul like the sea billows roll,

Db Ab   Eb7 Ab
Since Jesus came into my   heart.

Verse 2

   Ab
I have ceased from my wand'ring and going astray,

   Db   Ab
Since Jesus came into my heart.

And my sins, which were many, are all washed away,

   Bb7   Eb Ab Eb7
Since Jesus came into my heart.

Chorus 2   *Repeat Chorus 1*

Verse 3

         Ab
I'm pos - sessed of a hope that is steadfast and sure,

    Db   Ab
Since Jesus came into my heart.

And no dark clouds of doubt now my pathway obscure,

    Bb7   Eb Ab Eb7
Since Jesus came into my heart.

Chorus 3   *Repeat Chorus 1*

Verse 4

         Ab
There's a light in the valley of death now for me,

    Db   Ab
Since Jesus came into my heart.

And the gates of the city beyond I can see,

    Bb7   Eb Ab Eb7
Since Jesus came into my heart.

Chorus 4   *Repeat Chorus 1*

Verse 5

         Ab
I shall go there to dwell in that city, I know,

    Db   Ab
Since Jesus came into my heart.

And I'm happy, so happy, as onward I go,

    Bb7   Eb Ab Eb7
Since Jesus came into my heart.

Chorus 5   *Repeat Chorus 1*

Standing on the Promises

Words and Music by
R. Kelso Carter

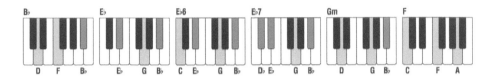

Verse 1

Bb
Standing on the promises of Christ my King!

Eb   Bb
Through eternal ages let His prais - es ring.

Glory in the highest I will shout and sing,

    Eb6   Eb7 Bb
Standing on the promis - es of God.

Chorus 1

Bb   Eb   Gm
Standing, stand - ing,

F   Bb   Eb Bb
Standing on the promises of God my Sav - ior.

        Eb
Standing, standing,

    Bb   Eb7 Bb
I'm standing on the promis - es of God.

Verse 2	**B**♭ Standing on the promises that cannot fail! **E**♭ **B**♭ When the howling storms of doubt and fear assail, By the living Word of God I shall prevail, **E**♭**6** **E**♭**7** **B**♭ Standing on the promis - es of God.
Chorus 2	*Repeat Chorus 1*
Verse 3	**B**♭ Standing on the promises of Christ the Lord, **E**♭ **B**♭ Bound to Him eternally by love's strong cord, Overcoming daily with the Spirit's sword, **E**♭**6** **E**♭**7** **B**♭ Standing on the promis - es of God.
Chorus 3	*Repeat Chorus 1*
Verse 4	**B**♭ Standing on the promises I cannot fall, **E**♭ **B**♭ List'ning every moment to the Spir - it's call, Resting in my Savior as my all and all, **E**♭**6** **E**♭**7** **B**♭ Standing on the promis - es of God.
Chorus 4	*Repeat Chorus 1*

Sweet By and By

Words by Sanford Fillmore Bennett
Music by Joseph P. Webster

There's a land that is fair - er than day,

Verse 1

      G   C   G
There's a land that is fairer than day,

                D
And by faith we can see it a - far.

     G   C   G
For the Father waits over the way

         C   G/D D   G
To prepare us a dwell - ing   place there.

Chorus 1

      G   D
In the sweet by and by,

     D7   G
We shall meet on that beautiful shore.

     G7/B C
In the sweet by and by,

     G   D7   G
We shall meet on that beautiful shore.

Verse 2

        G   C   G
We shall sing on that beautiful shore

                     D
The melodious songs of the blessed.

        G   C   G
And our spirits shall sorrow no more,

            C   G/D D G
Not a sigh for the bless - ing of rest.

Chorus 2   *Repeat Chorus 1*

Verse 3

        G   C   G
To our bountiful Father a - bove,

                     D
We will offer our tribute of praise

        G   C   G
For the glorious gift of His love

            C   G/D D G
And the blessings that hal - low our days.

Chorus 3   *Repeat Chorus 1*

Sweet Hour of Prayer

Words by William W. Walford
Music by William B. Bradbury

Verse 1

      D   **G**
Sweet hour of prayer, sweet hour of prayer,

      D   **A** **D/A** **A**
That calls me from a world of   care,

      D   **G**
And bids me at my Father's throne

      D   **A7 D**
Make all my wants and wish - es   known.

      A7/E D/F♯ G D
In sea - sons   of   dis - tress and grief,

      A7/E D/F♯ G D   **A**
My soul has   of - ten found re - lief,

      D   **G**
And oft escaped the tempter's snare

      D   **A7 D**
By thy return, sweet hour of   prayer.

Verse 2

      D   **G**
Sweet hour of prayer, sweet hour of prayer,

      D   **A** **D/A** **A**
Thy joy I feel, the bliss I   share

      D   **G**
Of those whose anxious spirits burn

      D   **A7 D**
With strong desire for thy re - turn.

      A7/E D/F♯ G D
With such I   has - ten to the place

      A7/E D/F♯ G D   **A**
Where God, my   Sav - ior, shows His face,

      D   **G**
And gladly take my station there,

      D   **A7 D**
To wait for thee, sweet hour of   prayer.

Verse 3

D   G
Sweet hour of prayer, sweet hour of prayer,

D   A D/A A
Thy wings shall my pe - ti - tion bear

D   G
To Him, whose truth and faithfulness

D   A7 D
En - gage the waiting soul to bless.

A7/E D/F♯ G D
And since He bids me seek His face,

A7/E D/F♯ G D   A
Believe His Word, and trust His grace,

D   G
I'll cast on Him my ev'ry care,

D   A7 D
And wait for thee, sweet hour of prayer.

Verse 4

D   G
Sweet hour of prayer, sweet hour of prayer,

D   A D/A A
May I thy conso - la - tion share,

D   G
Till from Mount Pisgah's lofty height

D   A7 D
I view my home and take my flight.

A7/E D/F♯ G D
This robe of flesh I'll drop,

A7/E D/F♯ G D A
And rise to seize the ev - er - lasting prize,

D   G
And shout, while passing through the air,

D   A7 D
"Fare - well, farewell, sweet hour of prayer."

Tell It to Jesus

Words by Jeremiah E. Rankin
Music by Edmund S. Lorenz

Melody:

Are you wea - ry, are you heav-y heart - ed?

G   D   G   B

C   C   E   G

D7   C   D   F♯   A

D   D   F♯   A

A7   C♯   E   G   A

Verse 1

| G | G/B C | G |
Are you wea - ry, are you heavy hearted?

D7   G
Tell it to Jesus, tell it to Jesus.

G/B   C   G
Are you griev - ing over joys de - parted?

D7   G
Tell it to Jesus a - lone.

Chorus 1

D   G   G/B
Tell it to Jesus, tell it to Je - sus,

C   G   D   A7   D   D7
He is a friend that's well - known.

G   G/B   C   G
You've no oth - er such a friend or brother,

D7   G
Tell it to Jesus a - lone.

Verse 2	G G/B C G Do the tears flow down your cheeks un - bidden?

G   G/B C   G
Do the tears flow down your cheeks un - bidden?

D7   G
Tell it to Jesus, tell it to Jesus.

G/B   C   G
Have you sins that   to men's eyes are hidden?

D7   G
Tell it to Jesus a - lone.

Chorus 2   *Repeat Chorus 1*

Verse 3

G   G/B C   G
Do you fear the   gath'ring clouds of sorrow?

D7   G
Tell it to Jesus, tell it to Jesus.

G/B C   G
Are you anx - ious   what shall be to - morrow?

D7   G
Tell it to Jesus a - lone.

Chorus 3   *Repeat Chorus 1*

Verse 4

G   G/B C   G
Are you trou - bled at the thought of dying?

D7   G
Tell it to Jesus, tell it to Jesus.

G/B C   G
For Christ's com - ing   kingdom are you sighing?

D7   G
Tell it to Jesus a - lone.

Chorus 4   *Repeat Chorus 1*

There Is a Fountain

Words by William Cowper
Traditional American Melody
Arranged by Lowell Mason

Verse 1

     Bb   Bb/D Eb   Bb
There is a foun - tain   filled with blood

                     F
Drawn from Immanuel's veins;

    Bb   Bb/D Eb   Bb
And sinners, plunged be - neath that flood,

Bb/D Eb6 Bb   F7   Bb
Lose _____ all their guilty stains:

          F   Bb Eb
Lose all their guilt - y stains,

    Bb   F
Lose all their guilty stains.

    Bb   Bb/D Eb   Bb
And sinners, plunged be - neath that flood,

Bb/D Eb6 Bb   F7   Bb
Lose _____ all their guilty stains.

PIANO CHORD SONGBOOK

Verse 2

Bb   Bb/D Eb   Bb
The dying thief re - joiced to see

F
That fountain in his day;

Bb   Bb/D Eb   Bb
And there may I, though vile as he,

Bb/D Eb6 Bb   F7   Bb
Wash _____ all my sins a - way;

F Bb Eb
Wash all my sins a - way,

Bb   F
Wash all my sins a - way.

Bb   Bb/D Eb   Bb
And there may I, though vile as he,

Bb/D Eb6 Bb   F7   Bb
Wash _____ all my sins a - way.

Verse 3

Bb   Bb/D Eb   Bb
Dear dying Lamb, Thy   precious blood

F
Shall never lose its pow'r,

Bb   Bb/D Eb   Bb
Till all the ran - somed Church of God

Bb/D Eb6 Bb   F7   Bb
Be _____ saved to sin no more:

F Bb Eb
Be saved, to sin no more,

Bb   F
Be saved to sin no more.

Bb   Bb/D Eb   Bb
Till all the ran - somed Church of God

Bb/D Eb6 Bb   F7   Bb
Be _____ saved, to sin no more.

Verse 4

    B♭   **B♭/D** **E♭**   **B♭**
E'er since, by faith, I   saw the stream

                  F
Thy flowing wounds sup - ply,

    B♭   **B♭/D** **E♭**   **B♭**
Re - deeming love has   been my theme,

B♭/D **E♭6** **B♭**   **F7** **B♭**
And _____ shall be till I die:

           F **B♭** **E♭**
And shall be till I die,

    B♭   **F**
And shall be till I die.

    B♭   **B♭/D** **E♭**   **B♭**
Re - deeming love has   been my theme,

B♭/D **E♭6** **B♭**   **F7** **B♭**
And _____ shall be till I die.

Verse 5

      B♭   **B♭/D** **E♭**   **B♭**
When this poor lisp - ing,   stamm'ring tongue

             F
Lies silent in the grave,

    B♭   **B♭/D** **E♭**   **B♭**
Then in a no - bler,   sweeter song

B♭/D **E♭6** **B♭**   **F7**   **B♭**
I'll _____ sing Thy pow'r to save:

          F   **B♭** **E♭**
I'll sing Thy pow'r to save,

    B♭   **F**
I'll sing Thy pow'r to save.

    B♭   **B♭/D** **E♭**   **B♭**
Then in a no - bler,   sweeter song

B♭/D **E♭6** **B♭**   **F7**   **B♭**
I'll _____ sing Thy pow'r to save.

When I Can Read My Title Clear

Words by Isaac Watts
Traditional American Melody
Attributed to Joseph C. Lowry

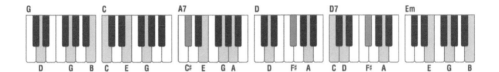

Verse 1

        G   C G
When I can read my title clear

             C G/B A7 D
To mansions in the skies,

    G   D7
I'll bid farewell to ev'ry fear

Em C   G/D C/D D7 G
And wipe my weep - ing _____ eyes,

              C G
And wipe my weeping eyes,

          C   G/B A7   D
And wipe my weep - ing eyes.

    G   D7
I'll bid farewell to ev'ry fear

Em C   G/D C/D D7 G
And wipe my weep - ing _____ eyes.

G   C   G
Should earth against my soul en - gage,

     C   G/B A7   D
And hellish darts be   hurled,

G   D7
Then I can smile at Satan's rage

Em C   G/D   C/D D7 G
And face a frown - ing _____ world,

                C   G
And face a frowning world,

        C   G/B A7   D
And face a frown - ing   world.

     G   D7
Then I can smile at Satan's rage

Em C   G/D   C/D D7 G
And face a frown - ing _____ world.

     G   C   G
Let cares like a wild deluge come,

        C   G/B A7 D
And storms of sor - row fall,

     G   D7
May I but safely reach my home,

Em C   G/D   C/D D7 G
My   God, my heav'n, my _____ all.

                C G
My God, my heav'n, my all,

        C   G/B A7 D
My God, my heav'n, my all,

     G   D7
May I but safely reach my home,

Em C   G/D   C/D D7 G
My   God, my heav'n, my _____ all.

Verse 4

        G   C   G
There shall I bathe my weary soul

         C   G/B A7 D
In seas of heav'n - ly   rest,

        G   D7
And not a wave of trouble roll

Em C   G/D   C/D D7 G
A - cross my peace - ful _____ breast,

                  C   G
Across my peaceful breast,

         C   G/B A7   D
Across my peace - ful   breast.

        G   D7
And not a wave of trouble roll

Em C   G/D   C/D D7 G
A - cross my peace - ful _____ breast.

There Is Power in the Blood

Words and Music by
Lewis E. Jones

Melody:

Would you be free from your bur - den of sin?

Verse 1

 Bb   Eb Bb
Would you be free from your burden of sin?

   F   Bb
There's pow'r in the blood, pow'r in the blood.

      Eb Bb
Would you o'er evil a victory win?

   F7   Bb
There's wonderful pow'r in the blood.

Chorus 1

    Bb   Eb   Bb
There is pow'r, pow'r, wonderworking pow'r

   F7   Bb
In the blood of the Lamb.

      Eb   Bb
There is pow'r, pow'r, wonderworking pow'r

   F7 Bb F7 Bb
In the precious blood of the Lamb.

Verse 2

B♭   E♭ B♭
Would you be free from your passion and pride?

  F   B♭
There's pow'r in the blood, pow'r in the blood.

      E♭ B♭
Come for a cleansing to Calvary's tide.

  F7   B♭
There's wonderful pow'r in the blood.

Chorus 2   *Repeat Chorus 1*

Verse 3

B♭   E♭ B♭
Would you be whiter, much whiter than snow?

  F   B♭
There's pow'r in the blood, pow'r in the blood.

      E♭ B♭
Sin-stains are lost in its life-giving flow.

  F7   B♭
There's wonderful pow'r in the blood.

Chorus 3   *Repeat Chorus 1*

Verse 4

B♭   E♭ B♭
Would you do service for Jesus, your King?

  F   B♭
There's pow'r in the blood, pow'r in the blood.

      E♭ B♭
Would you live daily His praises to sing?

  F7   B♭
There's wonderful pow'r in the blood.

Chorus 4   *Repeat Chorus 1*

'Tis So Sweet to Trust in Jesus

Words by Louisa M.R. Stead
Music by William J. Kirkpatrick

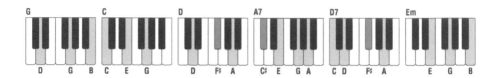

Verse 1

    G   C   G
'Tis so sweet to trust in Je - sus,

              D/F♯ A7/E D
Just to take Him at   His   Word.

    G   C   G
Just to rest up - on His prom - ise,

           C   G   D G
Just to know, "Thus saith the Lord."

Chorus 1

    G   D7 Em G   D
Jesus, Jesus, how I   trust Him,

    G   D/F♯ A7/E D
How I've proved Him o'er   and   o'er.

    G   G/B C   G
Jesus, Je - sus, precious Je - sus!

           C   G   D   G
O for grace to trust Him more!

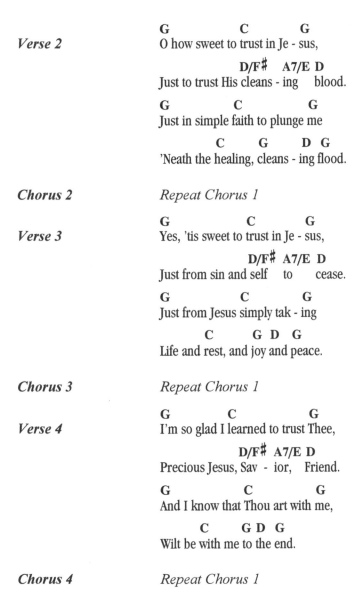

Verse 2

G   C   G
O how sweet to trust in Je - sus,

             D/F♯   A7/E D
Just to trust His cleans - ing   blood.

G   C   G
Just in simple faith to plunge me

           C   G   D G
'Neath the healing, cleans - ing flood.

Chorus 2

Repeat Chorus 1

Verse 3

G   C   G
Yes, 'tis sweet to trust in Je - sus,

             D/F♯ A7/E D
Just from sin and self   to   cease.

G   C   G
Just from Jesus simply tak - ing

           C   G D G
Life and rest, and joy and peace.

Chorus 3

Repeat Chorus 1

Verse 4

G   C   G
I'm so glad I learned to trust Thee,

             D/F♯ A7/E D
Precious Jesus, Sav - ior,   Friend.

G   C   G
And I know that Thou art with me,

        C   G D G
Wilt be with me to the end.

Chorus 4

Repeat Chorus 1

Turn Your Eyes Upon Jesus

Words and Music by
Helen H. Lemmel

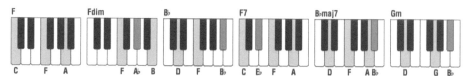

O soul, are you wea-ry and trou - bled?

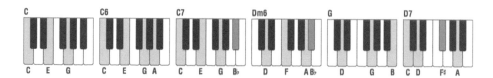

Verse 1

       F   Fdim F   Bb/D F7/C Bbmaj7 Gm
O soul, are   you wea - ry   and troub - led?

     F/C C F/C C6   C7   F
No light in the   dark - ness you see?

         Fdim F Bb   F   Dm6/F C/E
There's light for   a look at the Sav - ior,

C F G/F D7/F# C   G7   C
And life more a - bun - dant and free.

Chorus 1

     F   C   C7 Dm F7/C
Turn your eyes up - on Je - sus.

    Bb   Bm7b5 C
Look full in His wonder - ful   face,

F   C#dim7 Dm   F7/C Bb
And the things of earth will grow   strange - ly dim

Dm Db6 F/C C F/C C7   F
In   the   light of His glory and grace.

PIANO CHORD SONGBOOK

Verse 2

      F   Fdim F   Bb/D F7/C Bbmaj7 Gm
Through death in - to life ev - er - last - ing

    F/C   C F/C C6 C7   F
He passed, and we   fol - low Him there.

        Fdim F Bb   F   Dm6/F C/E
Over us sin   no more hath do - min - ion,

  C   F   G/F D7/F♯ C   G7   C
For more ___ than   con - qu'rors we are.

Chorus 2   *Repeat Chorus 1*

Verse 3

      F   Fdim F   Bb/D F7/C Bbmaj7 Gm
His word shall not fail you, He   prom - ised.

    F/C C   F/C C6 C7   F
Be - lieve Him, and all   will be well:

        Fdim F Bb   F   Dm6/F C/E
Then go to   a world that is dy - ing,

  C   F   G/F D7/F♯ C G7   C
His per - fect sal - va - tion to tell.

Chorus 3   *Repeat Chorus 1*

The Unclouded Day

Words and Music by
J.K. Alwood

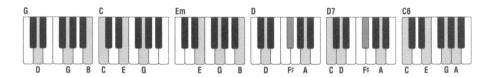

Verse 1

         G   C   G
O they tell me of a home far be - yond the skies,

             Em **D**
O they tell me of a home far a - way.

D7 **G**   C   G
O they tell me of a home were no storm clouds rise,

     G/B **C6** **G/D** **D7**   **G**
O they tell me of   an un - clouded day.

Chorus 1

 G
O the land of cloudless day,

             D
O the land of an unclouded sky,

D7 **G**   C   G
O they tell me of a home were no storm clouds rise,

     G/B **C6** **G/D** **D7**   **G**
O they tell me of   an un - clouded day.

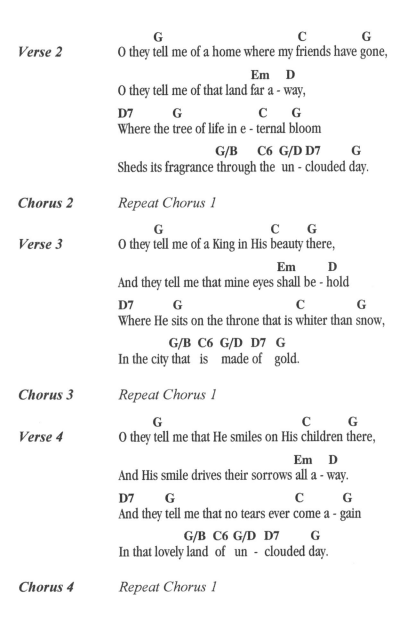

Verse 2

        G   **C**   **G**
O they tell me of a home where my friends have gone,

                Em   **D**
O they tell me of that land far a - way,

D7   **G**   **C**   **G**
Where the tree of life in e - ternal bloom

       G/B   **C6 G/D D7**   **G**
Sheds its fragrance through the un - clouded day.

Chorus 2   *Repeat Chorus 1*

Verse 3

        G   **C**   **G**
O they tell me of a King in His beauty there,

                 Em   **D**
And they tell me that mine eyes shall be - hold

D7   **G**   **C**   **G**
Where He sits on the throne that is whiter than snow,

     G/B **C6** **G/D** **D7** **G**
In the city that is   made of   gold.

Chorus 3   *Repeat Chorus 1*

Verse 4

       G   **C**   **G**
O they tell me that He smiles on His children there,

                 Em **D**
And His smile drives their sorrows all a - way.

D7   **G**   **C**   **G**
And they tell me that no tears ever come a - gain

     G/B **C6** **G/D** **D7**   **G**
In that lovely land of un - clouded day.

Chorus 4   *Repeat Chorus 1*

Wayfaring Stranger

Southern American Folk Hymn

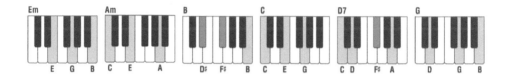

Verse 1

        Em
I am a poor wayfaring stranger

        Am   **B**
While trav'ling through this world of woe,

Yet there's no sickness, toil, nor danger

        Am   **Em**
In that bright world to which I go.

      C   **D7**   **G**
I'm going there to see my Father,

      C   **D7**   **Em**
I'm going there no more to roam;

I'm only going over Jordan,

     Am   **Em**
I'm only going over home.

Verse 2

Em
I know dark clouds will gather 'round me,

Am   B
I know my way is rough and steep;

But golden fields lie out before me

Am   Em
Where God's re-deemed shall ever sleep.

C   D7   G
I'm going there to see my mother,

C   D7   Em
She said she'd meet me when I come;

I'm only going over Jordan,

Am   Em
I'm only going over home.

Verse 3

Em
I'll soon be free from ev'ry trial,

Am   B
My body sleep in the church-yard;

I'll drop the cross of self-denial

Am   Em
And enter on my greatest re-ward.

C   D7   G
I'm going there to see my Savior,

C   D7 Em
To sing His praise for-ever-more;

I'm only going over Jordan,

Am   Em
I'm only going over home.

We'll Understand It Better By and By

Words and Music by
Charles A. Tindley

Tri - als   dark   on   ev - 'ry   hand,   and   we   can - not   un - der - stand...

Verse 1

   F   **C F7 B♭**   **F**
Trials dark on ev'ry hand, and we cannot under - stand

           C   **G7** **C7**
All the ways that God would lead us to that blessed Promised Land.

   F   **C F7 B♭**   **F**
But He'll guide us with His eye, and we'll follow till we die.

 B♭6 F   **C7**   **F**
We will understand it better by and by.

Chorus 1

F   **F7 B♭**   **F**
By and by, ___ when the morning comes,

     C   **G7** **C7**
When the Saints of God are gathered home,

   F   **F7 B♭**   **F**
We will tell the sto - ry   how we've over - come,

G7 **F**   **C7**   **F**
We will understand it better by and by.

Verse 2

        F   C   F7 B♭   F
Oft our cherished plans have failed, dis - ap - pointments have pre - vailed,

                                C   G7   C7
And we've wandered in the darkness, heavy hearted and a - lone.

        F   C F7 B♭   F
But we're trusting in the Lord and, ac - cording to His Word,

  B♭6 F   C7   F
We will understand it better by and by.

Chorus 2   *Repeat Chorus 1*

Verse 3

        F   C F7 B♭   F
Temp - tations, hidden snares of - ten take us un - awares,

                                C   G7   C
And our hearts are made to bleed for some thoughtless word or deed.

        F   C F7 B♭   F
And we wonder why the test when we try to do our best,

  B♭6 F   C7   F
But we'll understand it better by and by.

Chorus 3   *Repeat Chorus 1*

What a Friend We Have in Jesus

Words by Joseph M. Scriven
Music by Charles C. Converse

Verse 1

F　　Bb　F　　　Bb
What a Friend we have in Jesus,

F　　　　　　　C
All our sins and grief to bear.

F　　Bb　F　　Bb
What a priv - ilege to carry

F　　　　　C7　F
Ev'rything to God in　prayer!

C　　　　　　　　　F
O what peace we often forfeit,

Bb　F　　C7　F　C
O what needless pain we bear,

F　　Bb　F　　　Bb
All be - cause we do not carry

F　　　　　C7　F
Ev'rything to God in　prayer!

Verse 2

```
F      Bb  F           Bb
Have we tri - als and temp - tations?

F                 C
Is there trouble any - where?

F         Bb   F        Bb
We should nev - er be dis - couraged,

F                 C7  F
Take it to the Lord in   prayer.

C                        F
Can we find a friend so faithful

Bb       F    C7   F    C
Who will all our sor - rows share?

F    Bb    F       Bb
Jesus knows our ev'ry weakness,

F                 C7  F
Take it to the Lord in   prayer.
```

Verse 3

```
F     Bb   F         Bb
Are we weak and heavy laden,

F                   C
Cumbered with a load of care?

F         Bb   F        Bb
Precious Sav - ior, still our refuge,

F                 C7  F
Take it to the Lord in   prayer.

C                           F
Do thy friends despise, for - sake thee?

Bb    F    C7   F  C
Take it to the Lord in prayer.

F    Bb    F           Bb
In His arms He'll take and shield thee,

F                 C7  F
Thou wilt find a sol - ace there.
```

When the Roll Is Called Up Yonder

Words and Music by
James M. Black

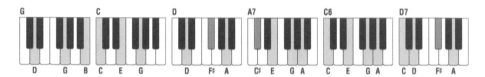

Verse 1

       G   G/B C   G
When the trumpet of the Lord shall sound, and time shall be no more,

            D/F♯ A7/E D
And the morning breaks, eternal, bright and fair,

       G   G/B C   G
When the saved of earth shall gather over on the other shore,

G/B C6 G   D7   G
And the roll is called up yonder, I'll be there.

Chorus 1

       G
When the roll is called up yonder,

       D7
When the roll is called up yonder,

       G   C
When the roll is called up yonder,

       G   D7   G
When the roll is called up yonder, I'll be there.

Verse 2

         G   **G/B**   **C**   **G**
On that bright and cloudless morning when the dead in Christ shall rise,

         D/F♯ A7/E D
And the glory of His resur - rec - tion   share;

       G   **G/B** **C**   **G**
When His chosen ones shall gather to their home beyond the skies,

G/B C6 G   **D7**   **G**
And   the roll is called up yonder, I'll be there.

Chorus 2   *Repeat Chorus 1*

Verse 3

       G   **G/B** **C**   **G**
Let us labor for the Master from the dawn till setting sun,

         D/F♯ A7/E D
Let us talk of all His wondrous love   and   care.

       G   **G/B** **C**   **G**
Then when all of life is over, and our work on earth is done,

G/B C6 G   **D7**   **G**
And   the roll is called up yonder, I'll be there.

Chorus 3   *Repeat Chorus 1*

When the Saints Go Marching In

Words by Katherine E. Purvis
Music by James M. Black

Verse 1

            E
Oh, when the saints go marching in,

                      B7
Oh, when the saints go marching in,

        E   **E7**   **A**
Oh Lord, I want to be in that number,

        E   **B7**   **E**
When the saints go marching in.

Verse 2

            E
Oh, when the sun refuse to shine,

                      B7
Oh, when the sun refuse to shine,

        E   **E7**   **A**
Oh Lord, I want to be in that number,

        E   **B7**   **E**
When the sun re-fuse to shine.

Verse 3	**E** Oh, when they crown Him Lord of all,

E

Verse 3   Oh, when they crown Him Lord of all,

             B7
Oh, when they crown Him Lord of all,

     E   **E7**   **A**
Oh Lord, I want to be in that number,

     E   **B7**   **E**
When they crown Him Lord of all.

     E

Verse 4   Oh, when they gather 'round the throne,

             B7
Oh, when they gather 'round the throne,

     E   **E7**   **A**
Oh Lord, I want to be in that number,

     E   **B7**   **E**
When they gather 'round the throne.

When We All Get to Heaven

Words by Eliza E. Hewitt
Music by Emily D. Wilson

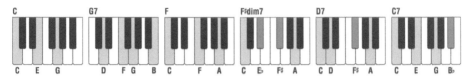

Verse 1

    C
Sing the wond'rous love of Jesus,

G7   **C**
Sing His mercy and His grace.

         F   **F#°7**
In the mansions bright and bless - ed,

C/G   **G7**   **C**
He'll pre - pare for us a place.

Chorus 1

        C
When we all get to heaven,

         D7   **G7**
What a day of re - joicing that will be!

    C C7 F
When we all see Jesus,

F#°7 C/G   **G7**   **C F C**
We'll sing and shout the victo - ry.

Verse 2

C
While we walk the pilgrim pathway,

G7   C
Clouds will overspread the sky.

              F $F\sharp^{\circ}7$
But when trav'ling days are o - ver,

C/G G7   C
Not a shadow, not a sigh.

Chorus 2   *Repeat Chorus 1*

Verse 3

C
Let us then be true and faithful,

G7   C
Trusting, serving ev'ry day.

                    F $F\sharp^{\circ}7$
Just one glimpse of Him in glo - ry

C/G   G7   C
Will the toils of life re - pay.

Chorus 3   *Repeat Chorus 1*

Verse 4

C
Onward to the prize before us!

G7   C
Soon His beauty we'll be - hold;

                F $F\sharp^{\circ}7$
Soon the pearly gates will o - pen;

C/G   G7   C
We shall tread the streets of gold.

Chorus 4   *Repeat Chorus 1*

Whispering Hope

Words and Music by
Alice Hawthorne

Soft   as the   voice   of   an   an - gel,

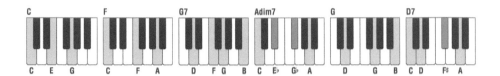

Verse 1

    C   F   C
Soft as the voice of an angel,

G7   C
Breathing a lesson un - heard,

                   F
Hope with a gentle per - suasion

C   G7   C
Whispers her comforting word:

                  Adim7 G7/B C
Wait till the dark - ness   is   over,

G   D7   G G7
Wait till the tempest is done.

C   F   C
Hope for the sunshine to - morrow,

          G7   C
After the shower is gone.

Chorus 1

G7   C   G7   C
Whispering hope, O how welcome Thy voice,

F   C   G7   C
Making my heart in its sorrow re - joice.

Verse 2

C   F   C
If, in the dusk of the twilight,

G7   C
Dim be the region a - far,

                         F
Will not the deepening darkness

C   G7   C
Brighten the glimmering star?

                     Adim7 G7/B C
Then when the night is   up - on us,

G   D7   G G7
Why should the heart sink a - way?

C   F   C
When the dark midnight is over,

              G7   C
Watch for the breaking of day.

Chorus 2   *Repeat Chorus 1*

Verse 3

C   F   C
Hope, as an anchor so steadfast,

G7   C
Rends the dark veil for the soul,

                         F
Whither the Master has entered,

C   G7   C
Robbing the grave of its goal.

                     Adim7 G7/B C
Come then, O come, glad   fru - ition,

G   D7   G G7
Come to my sad weary heart.

C   F   C
Come, O Thou blest hope of glory,

              G7   C
Never, O never de - part.

Chorus 3   *Repeat Chorus 1*

Whiter Than Snow

Words by James L. Nicholson
Music by William G. Fischer

Melody:

Lord Je - sus, I long to be per - fect - ly whole;

Verse 1

      A   E A   E7   A
Lord Jesus, I long to be perfectly whole;

       E   A   E7   A
I want Thee for - ever to live in my soul;

       A/C# D   A
Break down ev - 'ry idol, cast out ev'ry foe;

               E7   A
Now wash me and I shall be whiter than snow.

Chorus 1

E7   F#m   D A
Whiter than snow, yes, whiter than snow;

    D   A   E7   A
Now wash me, and I shall be whiter than snow.

PIANO CHORD SONGBOOK

Verse 2

      A   E   A   E7   A
Lord Jesus, look down from Thy throne in the skies,

          E A   E7   A
And help me to make a com - plete sacri - fice;

      A/C♯ D   A
I give up my - self and whatever I know,

                E7   A
Now wash me, and I shall be whiter than snow.

Chorus 2   *Repeat Chorus 1*

Verse 3

      A   E A   E7   A
Lord Jesus, for this I most humbly en - treat,

         E A   E7   A
I wait, bless - ed Lord, at Thy crucified feet;

      A/C♯ D   A
By faith, for my   cleansing, I see Thy blood flow,

               E7   A
Now wash me, and I shall be whiter than snow.

Chorus 3   *Repeat Chorus 1*

Verse 4

      A   E A   E7   A
Lord Jesus, be - fore You I patiently wait;

         E   A   E7   A
Come now and with - in me a new heart cre - ate;

      A/C♯ D   A
To those who have   sought Thee, Thou never saidst, "No."

               E7   A
Now wash me, and I shall be whiter than snow.

Chorus 4   *Repeat Chorus 1*

Will the Circle Be Unbroken

Words by Ada R. Habershon
Music by Charles H. Gabriel

I was stand-ing by my win-dow

Verse 1

         G   C   G
I was standing by my window on one cold and cloudy day,

                                  A7   D7
When I saw the hearse come rolling, for to take my mother a - way.

Chorus 1

         G   C   G
Will the circle be unbroken, by and by, Lord, by and by?

            C   G   D7   G
There's a better home a - waiting in the sky, in the sky.

Verse 2

         G   C   G
Oh, I told the undertaker, "Under - taker, please drive slow,

                                  A7   D7
For this body you are hauling, Lord, I hate to see her go."

Chorus 2   *Repeat Chorus 1*

Verse 3

         G   C   G
I will follow close behind her, try to hold up and be brave,

                                  A7   D7
But I could not hide my sorrow when they laid her in the grave.

Chorus 3   *Repeat Chorus 1*

Wonderful Grace of Jesus

Words and Music by
Haldor Lillenas

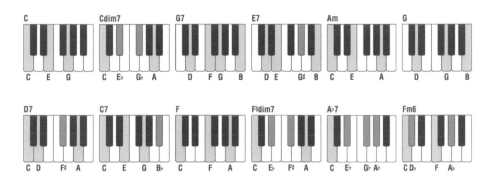

Verse 1

   C   Cdim7 C
Wonderful grace of Je - sus,

       G7 C E7
Greater than all my sin.

   Am
How shall my tongue describe it,

   G   D7   G G7
Where shall its praise be - gin?

   C   Cdim7 C
Taking away my bur - den,

     C7 F
Setting my spirit free,

Chorus 1

F#dim7   D7   C   Ab7
For the wonderful grace of Je - sus

C   G7 C
Reach - es me.

                                 G7
Wonderful, the matchless grace of Jesus,

C   G7
Deeper than the mighty rolling sea.

                     C
Higher than the mountain, sparkling like a fountain,

D7   G
All sufficient grace for even me.

C   G
Broader than the scope of my trans - gressions,

C   C7   F
Greater far than all my sin and shame.

 F#dim7   C   C/Bb F/A Fm6/Ab
O magnify the precious name of   Je - sus,

C   G7 C
Praise His name!

Verse 2

```
C              Cdim7 C
Wonderful grace of Je   -   sus,

        G7    C  E7
Reaching to all the lost.

Am
By it I have been pardoned,

G        D7    G   G7
Saved to the utter - most.

C                    Cdim7 C
Chains have been torn a - sun  -  der,

      C7    F
Giving me liber - ty.
```

Chorus 2   *Repeat Chorus 1*

Verse 3

```
C              Cdim7  C
Wonderful grace of Je   -   sus,

        G7      C  E7
Reaching the most de - filed,

Am
By its transforming power,

G        D7      G   G7
Making him God's dear child,

C                  Cdim7  C
Purchasing peace and heav  -  en

      C7    F
For all e - terni - ty.
```

Chorus 3   *Repeat Chorus 1*

Wonderful Peace

Words by W.D. Cornell
Music by W.G. Cooper

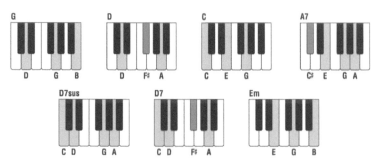

Verse 1

          G   D/A G/B C   G
Far a - way in the depths of   my spirit to - night

             A7   D7sus D7
Rolls a melody sweeter than psalm.

          G   D/A G/B C
In ce - lestial-like strains it   un - ceasingly falls

          G   D7   G
O'er my soul like an in - finite calm.

Chorus 1

      G   G/B C   G
Peace! Peace! Wonderful peace,

        Em   A7   D
Coming down from the Father a - bove.

          G   D/A G/B C
Sweep over my spir - it   for - ever, I pray,

        G   D7   G
In fathomless billows of love.

Verse 2

           G   D/A G/B C   G
What a treasure I have in   this wonderful peace,

              A7   D7sus D7
Buried deep in the heart of my soul.

          G   D/A G/B C
So se - cure that no pow - er can mine it away,

          G   D7   G
While the years of e - ternity roll.

Chorus 2   *Repeat Chorus 1*

Verse 3

        G   D/A G/B C   G
I am resting tonight in   this wonderful peace,

               A7   D7sus D7
Resting sweetly in Jesus' con - trol.

        G   D/A G/B C
For I'm kept from all dan - ger by   night and by day,

        G   D7   G
And His glory is flooding my soul.

Chorus 3   *Repeat Chorus 1*

Verse 4

        G   D/A G/B C   G
And me thinks when I rise to   that city of peace,

               A7   D7sus D7
Where the Author of peace I shall see,

        G   D/A G/B C
That one strain of the song which the   ransomed will sing,

        G   D7   G
In that heavenly kingdom will be,

Chorus 4   *Repeat Chorus 1*

Verse 5

        G   D/A G/B C   G
Ah, soul, are you here with - out   comfort or rest,

                 A7   D7sus D7
Marching down the rough pathway of time?

        G   D/A G/B C
Make Jesus your friend ere the shadows grow dark,

        G   D7   G
O ac - cept of this peace so sub - lime.

Chorus 5   *Repeat Chorus 1*

Wondrous Love

Southern American Folk Hymn

Melody:

What won-drous love is this, O my soul,

Verse 1

    Dm G Dm   F
    What wondrous love is this,

Am Dm F   Am
O my soul, O my soul,

F   Am   F
What wondrous love is this,

Am Dm
O my soul!

G   Am   Dm
What wondrous love is this

    Am   F   Dm
That caused the Lord of bliss

G Dm   F
To bear the dreadful curse

Am   Dm   Am
For my soul, for my soul,

    F   Am   Dm
To bear the dreadful curse for my soul!

Verse 2

G   Dm   F
What wondrous love is this,

Am   Dm   F   Am
O my soul, O my soul,

F   Am   F
What wondrous love is this,

Am   Dm
O my soul!

G   Am   Dm
What wondrous love is this

     Am   F   Dm
That caused the Lord of Life

G Dm   F
To lay aside His crown

Am   Dm   Am
For my soul, for my soul,

    F   Am   Dm
To lay aside His crown for my soul!

Verse 3

G Dm   F
To God and to the Lamb

Am   Dm   F   Am
I will sing, I will sing,

F   Am   F
To God and to the Lamb

Am   Dm
I will sing.

G   Am   Dm
To God and to the Lamb

    Am   F   Dm
Who is the Great I AM,

G   Dm   F
While millions join the theme,

Am   Dm   Am
I will sing, I will sing.

     F   Am   Dm
While millions join the theme, I will sing!

Verse 4

G Dm   F
And when from death I'm free,

Am   Dm F   Am
I'll sing on, I'll sing on,

F   Am   F
And when from death I'm free,

Am   Dm
I'll sing on.

G Am   Dm
And when from death I'm free,

   Am   F   Dm
I'll sing and joyful be,

G Dm   F
And through eterni - ty

Am   Dm   Am
I'll sing on, I'll sing on,

     F   Am   Dm
And through eterni - ty I'll sing on!

THE BEST
SACRED COLLECTIONS
FOR PIANO

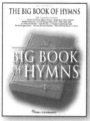

The Big Book of Hymns

An invaluable collection of 125 favorite hymns, including: All Hail the Power of Jesus' Name • Battle Hymn of the Republic • Blessed Assurance • For the Beauty of the Earth • Holy, Holy, Holy • It Is Well with My Soul • Just as I Am • A Mighty Fortress Is Our God • The Old Rugged Cross • Onward Christian Soldiers • Rock of Ages • Sweet By and By • What a Friend We Have in Jesus • Wondrous Love • and more.
00310510 P/V/G $17.95

The Best Gospel Songs Ever

80 of the best-loved gospel songs of all time: Amazing Grace • At Calvary • Because He Lives • Behold the Lamb • Daddy Sang Bass • His Eye Is on the Sparrow • His Name Is Wonderful • How Great Thou Art • I Saw the Light • I'll Fly Away • Just a Closer Walk with Thee • Just a Little Talk with Jesus • Mansion over the Hilltop • The Old Rugged Cross • Peace in the Valley • Will the Circle Be Unbroken • Wings of a Dove • more.
00310503 P/V/G $19.99

The Christian Children's Songbook

101 songs from Sunday School, all in appropriate keys for children's voices. Includes: Awesome God • The B-I-B-L-E • Clap Your Hands • Day by Day • He's Got the Whole World in His Hands • Jesus Loves Me • Let There Be Peace on Earth • This Little Light of Mine • more.
00310472 P/V/G $19.95

The Hymn Collection

arranged by Phillip Keveren

17 beloved hymns expertly and beautifully arranged for solo piano by Phillip Keveren. Includes: All Hail the Power of Jesus' Name • I Love to Tell the Story • I Surrender All • I've Got Peace Like a River • Were You There? • and more.
00311071 Piano Solo $11.95

Hymn Duets

arranged by Phillip Keveren

Includes lovely duet arrangements of: All Creatures of Our God and King • I Surrender All • It Is Well with My Soul • O Sacred Head, Now Wounded • Praise to the Lord, The Almighty • Rejoice, The Lord Is King • and more.
00311544 Piano Duet $10.95

Hymn Medleys

arranged by Phillip Keveren

Great medleys resonate with the human spirit, as do the truths in these moving hymns. Here Phillip Keveren combines 24 timeless favorites into eight lovely medleys for solo piano.
00311349 Piano Solo $10.95

Hymns for Two

arranged by Carol Klose

12 piano duet arrangements of favorite hymns: Amazing Grace • Be Thou My Vision • Crown Him with Many Crowns • Fairest Lord Jesus • Holy, Holy, Holy • I Need Thee Every Hour • O Worship the King • What a Friend We Have in Jesus • and more.
00290544 Piano Duet $10.99

Ragtime Gospel Hymns

arranged by Steven Tedesco

15 traditional gospel hymns, including: At Calvary • Footsteps of Jesus • Just a Closer Walk with Thee • Leaning on the Everlasting Arms • What a Friend We Have in Jesus • When We All Get to Heaven • and more.
00311763 Piano Solo $8.95

Seasonal Sunday Solos for Piano

24 blended selections grouped by occasion. Includes: Breath of Heaven (Mary's Song) • Come, Ye Thankful People, Come • Do You Hear What I Hear • God of Our Fathers • In the Name of the Lord • Mary, Did You Know? • Mighty to Save • Spirit of the Living God • The Wonderful Cross • and more.
00311971 Piano Solo $14.99

Sunday Solos for Piano

30 blended selections, perfect for the church pianist. Songs include: All Hail the Power of Jesus' Name • Be Thou My Vision • Great Is the Lord • Here I Am to Worship • Majesty • Open the Eyes of My Heart • and many more.
00311272 Piano Solo $15.99

More Sunday Solos for Piano

A follow-up to *Sunday Solos for Piano*, this collection features 30 more blended selections perfect for the church pianist. Includes: Agnus Dei • Come, Thou Fount of Every Blessing • The Heart of Worship • How Great Thou Art • Immortal, Invisible • O Worship the King • Shout to the Lord • Thy Word • We Fall Down • and more.
00311864 Piano Solo $14.99

Even More Sunday Solos for Piano

30 blended selections, including: Ancient Words • Brethren, We Have Met to Worship • How Great Is Our God • Lead On, O King Eternal • Offering • Savior, Like a Shepherd Lead Us • We Bow Down • Worthy of Worship • and more.
00312098 Piano Solo $14.99

HAL•LEONARD® CORPORATION

7777 W. BLUEMOUND RD. P.O. BOX 13819 MILWAUKEE, WI 53213

www.halleonard.com

P/V/G = Piano/Vocal/Guitar arrangements.

Prices, contents and availability subject to change without notice.

0715